AFG-5877

REFLECTIVE HISTORY SERIES

Barbara Finkelstein and William J. Reese, Series Editors

Moral Education in America:
Schools and the Shaping of Character from Colonial Times to the Present
B. EDWARD MCCLELLAN

Schooled to Work:
Vocationalism and the American Curriculum, 1876–1946
HERBERT M. KLIEBARD

The Failed Promise of the American High School, 1890–1995
DAVID L. ANGUS & JEFFREY E. MIREL

D0556034

Moral Education in America

Schools and the Shaping of Character from Colonial Times to the Present

B. Edward McClellan

DISCARD
LCCC LIBRARY

TEACHERS COLLEGE PRESS

Teachers College, Columbia University
New York and London

LC
286
.M38
1999

Published by Teachers College Press, 1234 Amsterdam Avenue, New York, NY 10027

Copyright © 1999 by Teachers College, Columbia University

All rights reserved. No part of this publication may be reproduced or transmitted in any form or by any means, electronic or mechanical, including photocopy, or any information storage and retrieval system, without permission from the publisher.

Library of Congress Cataloging-in-Publication Data

McClellan, B. Edward (Bernard Edward), 1939–
    Moral education in America : schools and the shaping of character
from colonial times to the present / B. Edward McClellan.
        p.   cm. — (Reflective history series)
    Includes bibliographical references (p.   ) and index.
    ISBN 0-8077-3821-2 (cloth : alk. paper). — ISBN 0-8077-3820-4
(paper : alk. paper)
        1. Moral education—United States—History.   2. Education—Social
aspects—United States—History.   I. Title.   II. Series.
LC311.M38   1999
370.11'4—dc21   99-13652

ISBN 0-8077-3820-4 (paper)
ISBN 0-8077-3821-2 (cloth)

Printed on acid-free paper
Manufactured in the United States of America

06   05   04   03   02   01   00   99   8   7   6   5   4   3   2   1

Contents

Foreword

"To get a good job, get a good education," said the well-known television commercial that first aired in the 1960s. A sign of the presumed connection between education and economic success in the postwar years, the commercial symbolized a momentous change in the way many Americans thought about schools. Preparing for adult responsibilities, including work, had long been part of the goals of America's public schools, especially since the dramatic expansion of vocational education after World War I. But throughout most of American history, even those citizens who believed that schooling had a positive influence upon adult material success embedded their ideas in a moral if not necessarily religious framework. Schools helped make a better world by teaching children to read and write, by helping immigrants to learn the English language and values of the majority culture, and by introducing the young through countless daily activities to what were seen as universally desirable and benevolent values: punctuality, hard work, respect for authority, and (not always the highest of virtues) academic success. Dutifully attending school and embracing its shared values was assumed to lead to a productive working life, or responsible parenthood—but until recently few educators, citizens, or politicians would have reduced the value of schooling to the familiar television jingle. In the long history of secularization in American education, something momentous had happened in the 1960s.

As B. Edward McClellan shows us, history has a tremendous role to play in explaining the fate of the teaching of moral, ethical, and religious values in the schools. Ours is not the first generation to fear that youth are in a state of moral decline, and that the family, school, and church have lost their power to shape the coming generation responsibly. History alone offers a widened perspective on how previous generations understood the nature and prospects of moral education. It alone helps students understand not only how the past evolved into the present, however unpredictably, but also what made the past and present both fascinating and distinctive. Far too many otherwise-informed scholars and citizens believe that only a resurgence of conservative values explains the evident popularity

vii

of such writers as William Bennett, former secretary of education in the Reagan administration and author of *The Book of Virtues*. On the contrary, as McClellan demonstrates, citizens in every generation from a host of backgrounds have debated what it means to behave morally and how adults should ensure the transmission of values to the young. In a pluralistic society, disagreement has never been in short supply.

An impressive variety of citizens living in modern America—unrivaled as a consumer-oriented, materialistic society—therefore continues to try to define the purposes of public schools and their possible role in building a good society. Like some dialectical imperative, a society dedicated to making money and defeating the enemies of capitalism wherever they exist has also generated concern for moral leadership, civic altruism, and the common good. The zealousness of those who want more school-to-work programs, which deepens the materialist ethos, is shared by those who want public aid for private church-based schools, the return of school prayer, and the restoration of adult authority, all of which advocates believe would shore up morality among the young. Reducing so much of education to the pursuit of material gain obviously leaves even the most conservative of Americans cold and nervous about the lost moral lessons once traditionally taught in the schools.

History cannot offer prescriptions for the ills of the present. But this volume effectively meets the aims of this book series by placing a subject of immediate, pressing public concern in an impressively broad framework. In an age of specialists who quite productively write books on relatively narrow subjects imbedded in short time periods, McClellan writes effortlessly about the grand themes and social practices in the history of moral education and character training over several centuries. He asks broad, difficult questions about the changing nature of education and character training over this time period. He avoids the usual pitfalls of the historian writing in this area, who yearns for a purer, better, usually imaginary past, a golden age where virtue once reigned.

Rather, McClellan wants to understand how Americans in the past understood the complexities of moral training, how it affected their ideas and social practices, and what difference it made in the lives of the young. History remains the one best way to see the dilemmas of the present in their broadest perspective, reminding us that some difficulties and challenges are unique to our time, while others are timeless.

William J. Reese
Madison, Wisconsin

Acknowledgments

This book is a significantly revised version of a volume originally published under the title *Schools and the Shaping of Character: Moral Education in America, 1607–Present* by the ERIC Clearinghouse for Social Studies/Social Science Education and the Social Studies Development Center at Indiana University. I am grateful to the clearinghouse and its director, John J. Patrick, for permission to publish this new edition.

Small parts of chapter 2 originally appeared in *Viewpoints* 51 (November 1975) and are included here with the permission of Indiana University.

My debts to colleagues are enormous. A. Stafford Clayton originally suggested that I study the history of moral education. John J. Patrick urged me to put the results of my study into a book, then waited patiently while I went about the task all too deliberately. I have enjoyed the assistance of Diana Bush Etiendi, Alex Duke, Jenness Hall, and Donald Moore. James C. Carper, Patricia A. Bauch, Michael J. Guerra, and Gary Ingersoll have generously shared materials with me. Ronald Cohen and Hamilton Cravens have been mentors and friends for many years and have offered much good advice on this project. Dean Donald Warren has been unstinting in his support. My greatest professional debt, however, is to William J. Reese— fellow traveler to countless research collections, sensitive critic, constant supporter, and good friend.

My personal debts are equally large. My parents taught me always to explore the moral dimensions of life's decisions. My sons, Douglas and Robert, not only gave up the company of their father far too often but also taught me much about moral education. But it is to my wife, Mary, that I owe the most. She has been the source of superb advice and unending support. This book is for her.

Preface

Few matters have captured the attention of a wider range of educators in the past quarter of a century than the place of moral education in American schools. Debates about how moral instruction ought to be provided—or whether it ought to be provided at all—have engaged many of the best minds in education and stirred a number of political controversies as well. Within academic circles the issues have received an extraordinarily thoughtful consideration from the likes of philosophers Andrew Oldenquist and Kenneth A. Strike; developmental psychologists Lawrence Kohlberg, Carol Gilligan, and William G. Perry Jr.; and curriculum specialists Gerald Grant and Kevin Ryan. The academic debates in turn have acquired a political urgency from the keen interest of the U.S. Department of Education, especially while under the leadership of William J. Bennett, and from the continuing activism of a variety of citizens' groups ranging from civil libertarians concerned about indoctrination to religious fundamentalists worried about modern relativism.

My own interest in this discourse began when first the journal *Viewpoints* and then a conference sponsored by the U.S. Department of Education invited me to provide some historical perspectives on moral education. The task proved to be a daunting one. Historians of education had not entirely ignored the topic, to be sure. They had, for example, carefully documented the moral earnestness of early textbooks, the stringent standards of conduct for teachers, and the evolving fashions in moral philosophy. Yet they had done little to trace the shifting institutional responsibilities for moral education or to explain changing notions about the nature of moral growth. More problematically, they had barely taken notice of the declining place of moral education in the twentieth-century school and college, leaving unexplored the very development that so many recent reformers have been trying to reverse.

The large gaps in previous historical scholarship have led me to a long exploration of original sources in an effort to find the broad patterns in the history of moral education in America. This book is a product of that exploration. It is written partly in the hope that it will provide perspective for those contemporary Americans who struggle with the problem of moral instruction, and partly in the hope that it will add to the body of scholarship in history of education and stimulate my colleagues in that field to extend the inquiry.

The dual purpose of the book has led me to make some decisions about emphases that require a word of explanation. First, I have confined my inquiry to formal efforts to provide moral education. Although sociologists believe that the rules and rhythms of school life—the hidden curriculum—may have more to do with shaping moral attitudes than formal instruction, it is formal instruction that has been the issue in recent debates. Second, I have given more attention to elementary and secondary schools than to institutions of higher learning. Here I have been influenced by the fact that Americans, especially in the last two centuries, have tended to view moral education as a process that takes place primarily during childhood or early adolescence. Third, in the interest of providing a broad perspective, I have traversed the long stretch of American history since the earliest English settlements, paying more attention to the predominant currents in each era than to the many divergences. Finally, I have dealt at greater length with recent events than with earlier ones. This is not, as it might at first seem, an attempt to emphasize the significance of recent events but rather an effort to provide a fuller treatment of developments that historians have tended to neglect.

Although this work seeks to inform contemporary discussion of moral education, it does not take a position in the debates. The question of what choices we ought to make is a matter better left to philosophers, theologians, and others whose task it is to define the good life and find ways to bring it into being. History serves this process best not by providing its own answers but rather by offering perspective and suggesting a rough sense of limits and possibilities. If this service falls short of insuring wisdom, it may at least encourage prudence and thereby assist those who must make the vital decisions on the proper place of moral education in American schools.

CHAPTER ONE

Moral Education in Early America

The vast array of European peoples who settled the American colonies brought with them both an extraordinary commitment to moral education and a rich variety of approaches to the task. The common commitment was rooted in the predominant Christian faith of the settlers; the variety was the product of both their diverse ecclesiastical and national backgrounds and the particular circumstances of their settlements. Especially in the early years, the various groups competed with each other, seeking not simply to perpetuate the faith among their own young but also to Christianize Native American populations and convert believers from other denominations.

French and Spanish settlers were the primary bearers of the Catholic tradition in the New World. With the help of highly educated and committed teaching orders, they successfully transplanted their faith to the American continent and made impressive missionary efforts among the Indians. Their strongest gains, however, lay outside the thirteen colonies that eventually banded together to create the United States, and their contributions to the mainstreams of American moral education were peripheral during the colonial era. Only a small band of English settlers in Maryland perpetuated a significant tradition of Catholic moral education in the thirteen colonies, and their efforts were often circumscribed by legal restrictions and overwhelmed by the preponderance of Protestant immigrants.[1]

Although the French and Spanish left important legacies in parts of Canada, Latin America, and what would become the western United States, it was Protestants from northern Europe, especially from Great Britain, who did the most to give moral education its character in the thirteen colonies. From the time of the first plantations in Virginia and Massachusetts, Protestantism in its various forms had an overwhelming influence on American life and culture.

The Early Years, 1607–1750

Of the groups who settled the New World in the seventeenth and early eighteenth centuries, the Puritans of New England left the fullest record

1

of both the purposes and the actual practices of moral education. Because they hoped that their experiment would set an example for the Old World, they were determined not only to establish a model Christian common-wealth but to document their successes. They were deeply committed to moral education and extraordinarily fearful that their children would drift away from the faith and culture. The fierce commitment was a product of both their Christianity and their special mission to the New World, their anxiety an expression of a fear that Christian values might not survive in the hostile environment of a wilderness society.

Puritans, who first settled New England in 1620, saw in moral educa-tion a way to keep religious orthodoxy alive, promote social harmony, encourage hard work, and spread the Christian faith to the heathen. Be-cause they were Calvinists who believed in predestination, they did not think that moral education could assure salvation for the nonelect, but they were convinced that it could encourage good behavior and create a soci-ety that would both glorify God and win divine blessings in the form of stable, harmonious, and prosperous communities.

Like most Europeans of the seventeenth century, Puritans assigned primary responsibility for moral education to the family, which by this point in history meant the immediate nuclear family. The laws of the Puri-tan colonies in New England specified that families should provide their children with an understanding of the doctrines of the faith and the laws and values of the society while also teaching them to read and to follow a useful occupation. In the eyes of the Puritans and other Christians of this era, religious and moral education were inextricably intertwined, and next to providing for the basic physical needs of the young, they were the most essential tasks of child rearing.

The most devout families among the Puritans used a whole range of occasions to instruct their children. They conducted family devotions at the beginning of each day; taught children to read and sometimes to write; drilled them in the church catechism; and exercised a careful, sometimes severe, discipline—all in an effort to produce children who would be pleas-ing in the sight of God and a credit to their families and communities.

The process began at an early age with the inclusion of children in the various forms of family devotions that were characteristic of the most pious Puritans. Even before children could read, they heard the prayers, Bible-reading, and psalm-singing of the parents. When they were able, the children themselves participated, often reading in turn carefully chosen passages from the Bible. One New Englander, Samuel Sewall, described in his diary the kind of devotions that were common in many Puritan house-holds: "This morning we read in course the 14, 15, and 16th Psalms. From the 4th v. of the 16th Ps. I took occasion to dehort mine from Christmas keeping [the Puritans considered Christmas a pagan celebration] and charged them to forbear. Hannah reads Daniel 6, and Betty, Luke 12."[2]

As children grew older, instruction became even more deliberate. The Puritan clergyman Cotton Mather, who reared his children in the late seventeenth and early eighteenth centuries, has left a vivid account of his family's unending efforts to assure the moral growth of children. Mather wrote of pouring "out continual Prayers and Cries to the God of all grace" for his children and of using a wide variety of occasions to instruct them in proper values:

> I begin betimes to entertain them with delightful Stories, especially *scriptural* ones. And still conclude with some *Lesson* of Piety; bidding them to learn that *Lesson* from the *Story*.
>
> And thus, every Day at the *Table*, I have used myself to tell a Story before I rise: and make the *Story* useful to the *Olive Plants about the Table*.
>
> When the Children at any time accidentally come in my way, it is my custome to lett fall some *Sentence* or other, that may be monitory and profitable to them.[3]

When parents were literate (and the majority of Puritan families had at least one literate parent), they taught their children to read the Scriptures. "The Scriptures," wrote one prominent Puritan, "are God's Law, they are Christ's Love-letters to His People, they are the Saints charter containing the Priviledges belonging to them. *Children* therefore should maintain a Diligent Constant Practice of *Reading the Holy Scriptures*, of regarding them as *the light of their feet, and lamp of their paths*."[4] Although the desirability of Scripture-reading was not the only reason for the development of mass literacy in Europe and the American colonies, it was a major force, especially among Protestants who thought that popular understanding of the Bible would keep their faithful from repeating what they regarded as priestly domination in the Catholic Church, a major issue during the bitter days of the Reformation.

Even more important than reading the Bible was instruction in the catechism. For most Puritan families, the catechism constituted the single most important element in formal moral instruction. Catechisms were definitive statements of the beliefs of particular denominations or congregations, and catechetical teaching (i.e., asking questions to test the child's knowledge of these beliefs) was perhaps the most widely used pedagogical device of the seventeenth and early eighteenth centuries.

Most catechisms began by leading children through a recitation of the basic doctrines of Christian faith. In New England, the shorter version of the Westminster Catechism opened with words that became familiar to generations of Reformed Christians and gave to Puritan children an early education in the fundamental tenets of their religion:

Q. 1. *WHAT is the chief end of man?*
A. Man's chief end is to glorify God, and enjoy him forever.
Q. 2. *What rule hath God given, to direct us how we may glorify and enjoy him?*
A. The word of god, which is contained in the Scriptures of the Old and New Testament, is the only rule to direct how we may glorify and enjoy him.
Q. 3. *What do the Scriptures principally teach?*
A. The Scriptures principally teach what man is to believe concerning God, and what duty God requires of man.
Q. 4. *What is God?*
A. God is a spirit, infinite, eternal, unchangeable in his being, wisdom, power, holiness, justice, goodness, and truth.[5]

The basic rules of moral conduct were taught in the context of religious doctrines, and they were rooted in scriptural commandments:

Q. 39. *What is the duty which God requires of man?*
A. The duty which god requires of man, is obedience to his revealed will.
Q. 40. *What did God at first reveal to man for the rule of his obedience?*
A. The rule which god at first revealed to man for his obedience was the moral law.
Q. 41. *Where is the moral law summarily comprehended?*
A. The moral law is summarily comprehended in the ten commandments.
Q. 42. *What is the sum of the ten commandments?*
A. The sum of the ten commandments is, to love the Lord our God with all our heart, with all our soul, and with all our strength, and with all our mind, and our neighbor as ourselves.[6]

Although families focused their educational efforts on their own children, they also had responsibility for the moral training of any young servants they employed or apprentices under their care. Even black slaves, where they existed in Puritan New England, received a measure of moral education, though the purpose was more to encourage subservience than to provide a full understanding of the faith and the culture.

In carrying out their educational responsibilities, mothers and fathers acted in concert, without a sharp differentiation in function. When clergymen and other Puritan leaders called for the education of the young, they addressed their remarks to both parents with the expectation that the two would reinforce each other's effort. By the late eighteenth century, moral education would be thought of as a special responsibility of the mother;

but before 1750, fathers were very heavily involved and probably even the primary providers of moral education, especially when sophisticated theological matters were involved.[7]

Similarly, Puritans did not differentiate between the values to be taught to boys and girls. Although families prepared girls and boys for different adult roles, they believed that a single morality applied to both. They not only instructed boys and girls together in their home, but taught them a single moral code. There was in Puritan society, to be sure, a subtle double standard when dealing with adult sexual behavior, but there is little evidence to suggest that parents taught children gender-specific moral values.[8]

After Puritan families had provided a grounding in moral and religious education, it was not uncommon for them to apprentice their children to other families. Unlike modern apprenticeship, which focuses on vocational skills alone, apprenticeship in this era involved education in the broadest sense of the term. Contracts drawn up between parents and masters and enforced by civil authorities invariably called for masters to insure the moral and religious education of the child as well as to provide occupational training and, in some cases, to teach the skills of reading, writing, and arithmetic.

As families went about the task of providing moral education for their children, at home and in apprenticeships, they were carefully supervised both by caring and curious neighbors and by civil authorities. Because Puritans tended to settle in tight-knit communities, privacy was virtually impossible, and families were under constant scrutiny, sometimes even by public inspectors who visited homes to insure that children were being properly cared for and educated. Where parents were judged inadequate they were subject not just to the scolding of unapproving neighbors but also to civil and even criminal penalties from the legal authorities.[9]

Legislative authority for dealing with parents who failed to educate their children came almost as early as settlement itself. In Massachusetts, for example, the general court passed a law in 1642 that expressed alarm about "the great neglect of many parents and masters in training up their children" and gave to town officials the power to fine negligent parents and place their children in apprenticeships where a proper education would be provided. The task of education was simply too important to leave in the hands of delinquent parents, and civil authorities did not hesitate to place orphans or neglected children in surrogate families or apprenticeships.[10]

The family and apprenticeship were the most important educational institutions in Puritan New England before 1750, but schools and churches played significant supporting roles in the process of moral education.

Schools were not universally available, but where they existed they reinforced the moral lessons first offered in the home. Their primary purpose was to teach the skills of literacy, with perhaps some instruction in writing and figuring, but they used materials that were suffused with religious and moral imagery. The instruction of the home was reinforced and developed in the hornbooks and primers used to teach children the alphabet and the elementary skills of literacy. Hornbooks were paddle-shaped pieces of wood covered by translucent horn which carried verses of Scripture or little poems such as:

> In *Adam's* Fall
> We sinned all

Primers contained simple verses, songs, and stories designed to teach at once the skills of literacy and the virtues of Christian living.[11]

For the vast majority of children in this era, schooling occupied only a small portion of their lives, if in fact it touched them at all. For a highly select minority, however, formal education extended into the Latin grammar school and the college. Here moral education went well beyond the rote learning of simple pieties. Especially in the colleges, students learned to interpret Scripture, understand theology, and apply knowledge of the liberal arts to the great moral, religious, and social questions of the day. Formal courses in ethics and theology provided a sophisticated understanding of the tenets of Christian faith while study of the classics gave students a thorough grounding in Western moral traditions.

The Puritan founders of Harvard College (1636) believed that educated rulers and clergymen would preserve the orthodoxy and set the moral tone of the society. Unlike some pietistic sects and many later evangelical denominations, they believed that all learning, secular as well as sacred, supported Christian faith—at least as long as students brought "right reason" to their study. In turn, the Puritans expected educated leaders to interpret the Scriptures to the less learned and to serve a broadly educational function on all matters related to morality.[12]

Unlike schools, churches played a relatively ill-defined role in moral education in this era, especially in New England where the catechism was taught primarily by the family. In this age before the Sunday school, churches often provided guidance to adults about moral education but generally left the task itself to other institutions. Some children might learn from sermons, and others—especially older children aspiring to higher education—might receive special instruction from ministers or elders, but even the religious education of the young was far more likely to be accomplished in the home than in the church.

Beyond such formal institutions as the family, apprenticeship, the school, and the church, children often acquired their values from the informal associations of community life. In a time when entire villages took a measure of responsibility for each child, it was common for youngsters to learn from neighbors as well as from extended kinfolk. Where communities were stable and pious, families welcomed the support they were likely to receive from other adults; where evils lurked, as in some port cities, upright families feared outside influences and tried to isolate their young from other adults.

Despite the tight network of formal institutions committed to moral education and the extraordinary public scrutiny of family life, Puritans went about the task of instruction with varying levels of intensity, ranging from near obsessiveness to surprising laxity—even neglect. As historian Philip Greven has argued, some families, who believed in a demanding God and a depraved humanity, took extraordinary steps to suppress any sign of willfulness in their children, enforcing a rigorous discipline that prepared their young for full obedience to God. Others, with a somewhat gentler view of both God and human nature, emphasized a more moderate control of the passions through the use of reason and a more measured discipline. And, as several recent historians have discovered, some families were able to evade official scrutiny altogether and allow their children to live instead by the dictates of a much less demanding folk culture, a culture that Puritan divines, try as they might, were never quite able to stamp out.[13]

Regional Variations

Although the Puritans have recorded the fullest account of moral education, it would be a mistake to assume that their approach was universal in the American colonies in the seventeenth and early eighteenth centuries. Not only did other groups in the southern and middle colonies have somewhat different traditions, but they also encountered different conditions, some of which had a profound effect on the kind of moral education they were able to achieve.

The starkest contrast to Puritan moral education was found in the Chesapeake colonies, especially Virginia. There harsh conditions made it impossible to establish the controlled and coordinated approach to moral education that Puritans had been able to achieve. The Anglicans who first settled Virginia shared with the Puritans a deep concern about the moral education of their young, even though they came to the New World for economic rather than religious reasons. From the first, their leaders feared the corrosive effects of the New World environment, and they quickly passed legislation to encourage the transmission of the society's religious and moral values to the young. In 1631, for example, the House of Burgesses passed a law stressing the importance of teaching the catechism:

> It is also thought fit, That upon every Sunday the minister shall half an hour or more before evening prayer examine, catechise, and instruct the youth and ignorant persons of his parish, in the ten commandments, the articles of the belief and in the Lord's prayer: And all fathers, mothers, masters and mistresses shall cause their children, servants or apprentices which have not learned the catechism to come to the church at the time appointed, obediently to hear, and to be ordered by the minister until they have learned the same: And if any of the said fathers, mothers, masters and mistresses, children, servants or apprentices, shall neglect their duties as the one sort in not causing them to come and the other in refusing to learn as aforesaid, they shall be censured by the courts in those places holden.[14]

Despite their strong feelings about moral education, however, Virginians found it difficult to match the Puritan achievement. The difficulty began with the structure of the family, where moral education was supposed to begin. For most of the seventeenth century, the family was an unstable institution in Virginia. Because of high death rates (malaria and other diseases made Virginia far unhealthier than New England), few nuclear families were able to form for long periods of time. As one parent or another died, children were left with the challenge of adjusting to stepparents, of being apprenticed to strange families, or of sinking into poverty with a single mother or father.[15]

High mortality rates and miserable health conditions were complicated by economic conditions. Especially in the early days of settlement, the task of clearing and farming land left mothers and fathers alike with little time to take children aside for either literary or moral instruction, a fact that is reflected in a literacy rate that was far lower than that of colonial New England. Although Virginians left few records of what actually happened in households, it is hard to imagine that they were able to give the kind of concerted attention to moral education that many pious Puritans were able to give.

Nor did the families of Virginia have the benefits of supporting institutions. Because they tended to live on scattered farms or plantations rather than in communities, Virginians could not depend on the support of close neighbors. The sheer distance between homesteads made it difficult to sustain churches, build schools, or even create informal networks of kinfolk and neighbors. Families could and often did place their children in apprenticeships, but this frequently meant simply sending the young from one struggling family to another.

Most families were undoubtedly able to convey to children some sense of their fundamental values, and a few well-to-do settlers had the where-withal to provide an elementary education to their children at home (often with the help of a tutor) and even to send them to England for a secondary and collegiate education. Yet even the wealthy struggled against impressive odds in the years before 1750, since Virginia had few elementary or secondary schools and only one college (William and Mary, which was created in 1693).

Despite the obstacles they faced, Virginians remained deeply concerned about the education of their children in this era. If they did not have the time to keep the kind of elaborate diaries that New Englanders kept, they nonetheless left a record of their educational vision in the wills they wrote. Studies of the wills of Virginia (and of its sister Chesapeake colony, Maryland) show that a substantial number of settlers made provision for the continuing education of their children from the very first, sometimes designating funds to hire individual tutors, other times leaving an endowment for a local school.[16]

As other Protestant settlers followed the Virginians and the Puritans to the New World, they each established slightly different traditions in moral education. The Quakers of Pennsylvania, for example, placed less emphasis on literacy and Bible reading than the Puritans but expected parents to exercise firm discipline and to teach children the catechism and the basic values of Quaker society.[17] In general, other southern settlers tended to mimic the Virginia experience, while those who settled the middle colonies were more like the Puritans. Despite the differences, however, settlers across the colonies in the years between 1607 and 1750 shared many assumptions about moral education. Not only did they exhibit a common anxiety about the task, but they developed many similar approaches. Everywhere, settlers expected the family to be the primary purveyor of moral values, with apprenticeship, schooling, and the church serving as important supplementary institutions. Everywhere, they believed that religion and morality were linked, and almost always they used the catechism as the primary pedagogical tool for teaching the essential truths of the society.

The Softening Tone of Moral Education, 1750–1820

Americans of the late eighteenth and early nineteenth century retained many of the forms of moral education that had developed in the early colonial years, but they made some subtle changes as well and gave to the process a decidedly different tone, especially in the stable and prosperous areas along the Atlantic coast. Here life had acquired a comfortable, almost casual quality about it, and moral education began to lose some of the tense rigidity that early settlers had given it.

At the root of the new moral tone was the extraordinary stability of family and community life in the towns, cities, and plantations along the eastern seaboard where most Americans still lived. Communities were both more prosperous and more confident of their ability to accommodate change without losing their moral bearings. Despite an increase in both social and geographical mobility, change in these years took place in the context of a stable, hierarchical society, where a sense of mutual obligation governed the relationships of social classes and where informal networks of people who knew each other over long periods of time supplied a mechanism to preserve the basic values of the society.[18]

The new stability was as apparent in the plantation South as in the northern and middle colonies. Although the South still lacked the tight-knit communities of the other regions, both plantation life itself and networks of kinfolk and neighbors served many of the same functions as the more concentrated towns and neighborhoods to the north. Backcountry discontent and slavery added potential sources of disorder, but for the most part, eastern elites exercised a firm control.

In this atmosphere of relative stability, both parents and civil authorities developed a strong confidence in the corrective and educative powers of community life. They found in communities—or what substituted for communities in the South—a web of institutions and associations that would reinforce each other in the task of moral education. Where one agency failed, others were in place to take up the cause. Children who defied parents could expect to encounter kinfolk, neighbors, or civil authorities who would assume the tasks of discipline and moral education. Moreover, since most children were expected to stay in their home communities, at least until early adulthood, education could be achieved slowly over a relatively long period of time.

As Americans gained confidence in their society, many of them lost some of their hard-edged religious orthodoxy and moral rigidity. In most cases, this did not imply a rejection of religion itself but rather a less theologically rigorous approach to it. Nor did it indicate an abandonment of traditional values. As the aphorisms of Benjamin Franklin and others indicate, the fundamental rules had not changed. Now, however, most Americans had enough confidence in the educative powers of a stable society that they could countenance an occasional bending of the rules. Thus, Franklin could write about the importance of chastity while conducting an occasional affair with a mistress. In this atmosphere of confidence and stability, such deviations neither presaged individual lives of debauchery nor threatened the harmony of the society. Communities were too strong, and their corrective powers too well-established.

Nowhere was the new tone more obvious than in the family itself, where all across the colonies a more affectionate and egalitarian structure challenged the rigid patriarchal forms so characteristic of the seventeenth and early eighteenth centuries. As relationships changed, a growing number of parents adopted more moderate approaches to child rearing. Heavily influenced by the writings of John Locke, child rearing manuals of the day emphasized the malleability of human nature, the importance of play, and the value of allowing children to grow up more slowly.[19]

A few families used these new doctrines to justify a surprisingly permissive approach to child rearing and education. Mostly from elite social circles, these families often embraced the Enlightenment vision of a distant, beneficent God and a humanity fully capable of shaping its ultimate destiny. Instead of suppressing or sharply controlling the willfulness of their young, these genteel Americans encouraged a strong measure of self-assertiveness. They expected their young to acquire an appropriate commitment to public duty, but they also allowed them to develop the kind of self-display and freewheeling social life that was characteristic of the aristocratic classes, especially in the South.[20]

A far greater number of families, however, embraced an approach that lay somewhere between harsh seventeenth-century methods and the permissive habits of the genteel. Unlike the permissive elites, these families did not encourage self-assertiveness or self-display, nor did they challenge traditional values. Yet they accepted playfulness as a natural part of growing up, and they were undisturbed by occasional deviations from the usual moral norms. Moreover, instead of emphasizing a rigorous early training, which had been common in the seventeenth century, they allowed education to unfold slowly over a long period of time. Thus, it was not uncommon in this era for youngsters as old as fifteen and sixteen to be enrolled in elementary school.

As this moderate approach to child rearing came to be the predominant approach in the late eighteenth and early nineteenth centuries, the educational roles of mothers and fathers began very gradually to diverge. Now, instead of viewing parents as essentially interchangeable agents in the process of moral education, Americans began to assign special responsibilities to the mother. This was especially the case in those towns and cities where growing numbers of professionals, merchants, and craftsmen worked away from the home and where servants of "good breeding" were more difficult to find. In this environment women were valued less for the practical support they could give to family businesses—although that role continued—and more for the nurture they could provide for their children. Perhaps making a virtue out of necessity, Americans began to ascribe to women special moral qualities and to give them primary responsibility within the family for the moral nurture of the child.[21]

The subtle redefinition of educational responsibilities promoted an equally subtle gendering of moral education, with girls increasingly being prepared for a special maternal role while boys were schooled for work outside the home. What Daniel Blake Smith found on the great plantations of the South was true in varying degrees throughout late eighteenth- and early nineteenth-century America: There the most widely read books on the subject exhorted "women to develop their natural traits of modesty, meekness, compassion, affability, and piety," while men were expected to prepare for "more competitive political and economic arenas, which distracted them from spiritual and altruistic pursuits."[22] From this point forward in American history until well into the twentieth century, women would be thought of as the special conservators of morality and piety in the society, and moral education would have about it a decidedly feminine cast.

Although their role in child rearing grew in the years after 1750, mothers were far from alone in their efforts to provide moral education to the young. Indeed, Americans showed an increasing tendency to allow families to delegate a portion of their educational responsibilities to a variety of other people and institutions. Because they shared a strong trust in the strength and moral soundness of their communities, Americans of the day countenanced many different approaches to moral education, including ones that diffused functions across a number of agencies. On the plantations of the South, for example, parents often left religious education entirely in the hands of the church and hired tutors to round out the moral and academic education of their children.

In the North, churches and schools acquired new educational responsibilities. Parents were increasingly willing to give churches a substantial role in moral education, entrusting them with the teaching of the catechism and supporting the creation of Sunday schools for the moral training of orphans and other troubled or dangerous youngsters. Similarly, they not only built schools in large number, but they expected them to play a substantial role in moral education.

In the years immediately following the American Revolution, a small group of intellectuals and statesmen sought to expand the role of the school even more dramatically. Worried about the ability of the new nation to survive in the face of parochialism and factional disputes, men like Thomas Jefferson, lexicographer Noah Webster, and Philadelphia physician Benjamin Rush proposed the creation of state systems of public schools that would teach "republican values" and encourage loyalty to the new nation.

They placed special emphasis on the teaching of "virtue," which they defined roughly as the willingness to set aside purely selfish motives and work for the good of the larger society. No longer inclined to trust the haphazard efforts of families and communities, they sought a more systematic education that would promote larger loyalties.[23]

Despite strong and persistent efforts, however, the warnings of these political and intellectual leaders fell largely on deaf ears. Few Americans shared their deep anxieties about national cohesion, and fewer still were willing to relinquish their control over the education of their children. Thus, even after the Revolution and the political struggles that followed it, Americans continued to place control of education in the hands of families and communities, who in turn continued to approach moral education with a confidence born of stability, prosperity, and an increasingly benevolent view of human nature.

Developments in higher education paralleled the changes taking place in the moral education of the masses of children. At Harvard, William and Mary, Yale, and other colleges, instructors and students alike often drifted away from religious orthodoxy and lost the grim earnestness of their early colonial predecessors. Although all of these institutions continued to operate within a general Christian framework, they were increasingly open to religious disputes and to the more secular ideas of the Enlightenment. Especially after the middle of the eighteenth century, many students showed a declining interest in the fine points of theology and a far greater concern for purely secular matters. At most colleges, the ideas of the Enlightenment led to alterations in the curricula with courses in science and political thought taking a place alongside the more traditional offerings in theology and ethics.

The new moral tone in education was never universal in the years between 1750 and 1820. Along parts of the frontier and in places most deeply affected by religious revivalism, the intense qualities of seventeenth-century moral education survived. This was especially the case where Methodists and Baptists challenged older, more moderate denominations at the end of the eighteenth and beginning of the nineteenth century. Many of these Christians of evangelical persuasion employed rigorous approaches to child rearing and moral education, and they offered strong resistance to the seeming relaxation of standards by many other Americans. Moreover, newer groups of settlers, especially the pietistic sects in the middle parts of the country, often sided with evangelical groups and fought what they also saw as an erosion of Christian values.

These exceptions notwithstanding, the predominant tone of moral education from 1750 to 1820 was clearly moderate. Families continued to teach traditional values, and the vast majority of parents still saw the world in fundamentally Christian terms. Yet most of them exhibited little of the anxiety characteristic of an earlier age. Confident in themselves and their communities, they embraced an approach to moral education that allowed the process to unfold slowly in a variety of formal and informal ways. In the end, they believed, strong communities of concerned adults would find the appropriate means to perpetuate the society's values and to produce men and women of faith and virtue.

CHAPTER TWO

The Nineteenth-Century Revolution in Moral Education, 1820–1900

The stability that gave eighteenth-century moral education its predominantly moderate tone survived both the American Revolution and the War of 1812, but it eroded dramatically after 1820 as the United States began to undergo a series of political, economic, social, and demographic transformations. These transformations brought enormous new opportunities to the young nation, but they also undermined the social arrangements that had allowed Americans to take a moderate position on moral education in the years between 1750 and 1820.

The changes that transformed American life were the product of complex impulses, some of which had begun to emerge as early as the Revolution itself. The collapse of the old order was perhaps most apparent in the world of politics, where the rule of a propertied elite was replaced by an extension of the suffrage to virtually all adult white males. Nothing symbolized the vital new popular democracy so much as the 1828 election of President Andrew Jackson, the model of a self-made man, who argued that the affairs of state could be carried out by common folk as easily as by the aristocrats who had dominated previous administrations.

The creation of popular rule was accompanied by a vast quest for new freedom and opportunity. In search of both individual liberty and economic advancement, Americans of the nineteenth century created new forms of enterprise, opened western lands for settlement, greatly expanded cities, railed against strong governmental control of their affairs, and fashioned an array of new social arrangements. Taken together, these changes contributed to what Robert Wiebe has characterized as a dramatic "opening" of American society. Traditional sources of social order—stable hierarchical social structures, patterns of cultural and political deference, webs of extended kinships, and tight-knit communities—weakened as images of control and orderly change gave way to visions of movement and opportunity.[1]

The quest for popular rule and liberty, however, defined only one part of the transformation of American life. Even as nineteenth-century Ameri-

15

cans worked to clear away the institutional restraints of colonial society, they moved in precisely the opposite direction in the realm of morals and personal behavior, abandoning the relaxed style of the eighteenth century in favor of an insistence on rigid self-restraint, rigorous moral purity, and a precise cultural conformity. Although the range of religious doctrines widened in these years, a distinctly evangelical temperament pervaded the society, making it closer in tone to the seventeenth century than to the late eighteenth.

The combination of impulses toward freedom and moral rigidity was less a cultural contradiction than a reflection of the belief that the growing absence of external, institutional restraints required the development of strong internal controls. In the minds of nineteenth-century Americans, the price of liberty was rigorous self-discipline and upright personal conduct.[2] Accordingly, men and women of the day approached moral questions with an intensity that would have shocked Benjamin Franklin and his contemporaries.

This dual quest for liberty and self-restraint was strongest in the years between 1820 and 1865, an era when it was symbolized by Jacksonian democracy on the one hand and by an array of crusades for moral reform on the other. Both impulses weakened with the Civil War and Reconstruction, but the commitments forged in the earlier era continued to define the basic terms of American life until the very end of the century.

Social Change and the Transformation of Child Rearing

The new intensity about morality manifested itself in a variety of dramatic ways—in the revival of evangelical Christianity, in the emergence of utopian and moral reform movements, and in the creation of an entirely new genre of moralistic sentimental literature. Change was also apparent in the more obscure efforts of countless families and communities to prepare their young for a life in the open, restless, and mobile society of the nineteenth century.

What most sharply differentiated the challenge of child rearing in this era was the need of parents to prepare their young for a life away from home. Nineteenth-century Americans were no longer able to assume that their children would stay in their home communities where caring elders would nurture them into responsible adulthood. They were forced to contemplate the possibility that youngsters would move away at an early age, truncating the usual period of education and subjecting themselves to the temptations of the world with only strangers to provide support and guidance.

The growing tendency of youngsters to leave home was a part of a larger pattern of mobility that began in the years around the American Revolution. Not only did Americans begin to move more often, they began to move greater distances.[3] Most often they moved as families or groups of families, but increasingly children followed their own individual paths toward new opportunities, leaving behind the familiar surroundings and highly personal connections of their home communities.

Two forces were at work in the surge of mobility between the Revolution and Civil War. The first was an explosion of opportunities brought about by westward expansion, economic growth, the burgeoning of commercial cities, and a process of democratization that opened avenues of advancement to social groups and classes that had never before dreamed of such possibilities. The second was a weakening of old attachments at home. A gradual decline in the family economy was of particular importance in this process. The once-secure places for children on diversified family farms and in small businesses began to disappear as larger-scale manufacturing and commercial enterprises gained competitive advantage. Parents were less and less able to promise a permanent economic niche for all their children, and the most insecure of them understood that their young would have to seek opportunity elsewhere.[4]

As young Americans began to pursue opportunities away from home, communities lost the capacity to educate their children at a slow and measured pace. Now if values were to be taught and behavior shaped, the task had to be accomplished well before the child could move beyond the protective environment of the home community into a world of strange people, restless activity, and alluring evils. Elders abandoned the relaxed attitudes of the prerevolutionary era and developed far more rigid and insistent approaches to moral education.

Underlying the new anxiety about moral education was a widespread fear about what lay beyond the home community. Americans accustomed to centering their lives around familiar and stable local structures found it easy to think the worst about the world outside. Easterners heard and believed rumors that the frontier was a place of instability, incivility, and violence. Small-town Americans thought even worse of cities, where drinking, gambling, whoring, and other kinds of immorality were reputed to be rife and where the tight personal restraints of community life were impossible. If youngsters found excitement in the opportunities of far-away places, their elders were often more impressed by the dangers.

As Americans contemplated the prospect of sending their children into these dangerous worlds, they gave to moral education an urgency it had often lacked in the eighteenth century. They also gave it a quality of definition and systematization it had never had in the colonial period. Children increasingly acquired their values in common ways through agencies assigned special responsibility for their education, moving almost in lock-step through early family training and schooling on their way to adulthood.

The New Importance of Early Education

The most obvious dimension of this new definition was time. Moral educa-tion, once a task that extended well into adulthood, now assumed the tem-poral limits of childhood itself. Even a remote chance that youngsters might leave home in their middle teens inclined anxious elders to assure that proper moral training was accomplished early, usually in the first twelve years of life. To fail in those years opened up the possibility that children would forever lose the chance to learn the proper values. Parents and neigh-bors could be trusted to teach the right values and enforce the proper be-haviors, but few nineteenth-century Americans believed that strangers in distant towns and cities would exhibit the same level of concern.

The importance of early moral education quickly became an article of faith in the early nineteenth century. "The germs of morality," wrote the public school champion Horace Mann, "must be planted in the moral na-ture of children, at an early period of their life." To fail in those critical years was to miss an opportunity unlikely to be recaptured except in the extraor-dinary environment of the penitentiary, the reformatory, or the asylum. To succeed, on the other hand, was to equip the child to lead a life of vir-tue in a world full of temptations and relatively devoid of institutions ca-pable of gently correcting wayward men and women. The goal of early moral training, wrote Mann, was to make the child like "those oaks" that "preserve their foliage fresh and green, through seasons of fiery drought, when all surrounding vegetation is scorched to a cinder."[5] Combining a faith in the malleability of the child with a pessimism about the reform-ability of adults, nineteenth-century Americans simply assumed that the alteration of early habits—good or bad—was "as little probable as that 'the Ethiopian should change his skin, or the leopard his spots.'"[6]

By imposing narrow temporal limits on moral education, Americans forced a sharpening of the lines of institutional responsibility as well. No longer could society afford the variegated patterns and informal methods of the more casual era between 1750 and 1820. A process so urgent and so compressed by time required the intense, specialized efforts of designated agencies. Accordingly, nineteenth-century Americans made moral educa-tion the special responsibility of two institutions especially adaptable to the task of offering intensive training to the very young—the family and the school. "The most dangerous transition in a youth's life," declared one educator of the day,

> is that which carries him from the authoritative control of the family and the school to the responsibility of untried liberty. The shores of this perilous strait of human life are strewn with wrecked manhood. The home-life and the school-life of the child should prepare him for this transition to freedom by effective training in self-control and self-guidance, and, to this end, the will must be disciplined by an increasing use of motives that quicken the sense of right and make the conscience regal.[7]

Beyond the efforts of these two agencies, early nineteenth-century Americans found few institutional resources to guard against the ever-present temptations of an unstable world. Consequently, they placed extraordinary demands on both the family and the school, and, in the process, gave a sharp definition to the institutional context of moral education.

The Special Role of the Mother

By all standards, primary responsibility came to rest with the family. "Having ordained that man should receive his character from education," proclaimed one parents' guide of the 1830s, "it was ordained that early instruction should exert a decisive influence on character, and that during this important period of existence, children should be subject to the charge of their parents."[8] Responsibility for moral education was hardly new to the family, but in the colonial era the family had been only one of many institutions involved in the task. If it failed, other agencies could be expected to assume the burden somewhere along the long line that stretched from infancy to adulthood. Now, however, the family was singled out as the primary influence during the short years of childhood when character was formed. Its failure was often thought to mean a lifetime of moral failure for the child.

As the family assumed an ever-growing role in moral education, the duties of the mother expanded even further. Now, as more and more fathers worked away from the home, mothers came to bear almost exclusive responsibility for the moral nurturing of the child. As the member of the family who had the closest and most continuous associations with the child during the formative years, her role was now critical and her influence virtually irreplaceable.

The special role of the mother came to be highly celebrated in the nineteenth century. Ladies' magazines, popular literature, and a wide range of child rearing manuals both proclaimed the duties of the mother and offered a wealth of advice about how to insure the proper education of their children. "By the plan of creation and the providence of God," declared Dr. Daniel Drake, a Cincinnati physician and popular speaker on domestic education, "it is the peculiar duty of the mother, to watch over her child for many of the first years of its life, and on her more than the father rests the responsibility."[9] In the mother's hands, warned Samuel Goodrich, author of children's literature and parents' manuals, lay the greatest power for shaping the character of the child:

> You have a child on your knee. Listen a moment. Do you know what that child is? It is an immortal being, destined to live forever! It is destined to be happy or miserable! And who is to make it happy or miserable? You—the mother! You who gave it birth, the mother of its body, are also the mother of its soul for good or for ill. Its character is yet undecided; its destiny is placed in your hands. That child may be a liar. You can prevent it. It may be a drunkard. You can prevent it. It may be a thief. You can prevent it. It may be a murderer. You can prevent it . . . It may descend into the grave with an evil memory behind and dread before. You can prevent it. Yes, you, the mother can prevent all these things. Will you, or will you not?[10]

Such rhetoric placed a heavy burden on mothers, giving them at once new powers in the domestic realm and extraordinary responsibilities for a task that had once been broadly shared by a variety of people within the society. As mothers went about their new duties, they did much to establish the moral standing of their families in the community. By extension women, more than men, were recognized as moral leaders within communities. The association between morality and femininity grew even sharper in this era as the world of business came to be identified as a rough-and-tumble masculine arena.

Mothers were expected to go about the task of moral education by exhibiting a constant Christian virtue in their own lives and through daily readings and exhortations to children designed to increase piety and teach proper conduct. Unlike evangelicals of the colonial era, nineteenth-century mothers tended to view their children as neither inherently good nor inherently evil but rather as malleable, and they worked less to break the wills of their young than to cultivate by example and instruction a powerful inner desire for virtuous living. Consequently they were expected to be gentle and cheerful and to create strong associations between virtue and happiness.[11]

Mothers gradually abandoned the catechetical approaches so common in the colonial era, paying less attention to fine theological distinctions than to general moral rules. Given the length of time available to them and the enormity of their task, the inculcation of simple moral truths and the shaping of a powerful conscience seemed more important than a careful schooling in the intricacies of doctrine. What counted in a world where children would grow up to face temptations without the support of traditional networks of families and friends was a certain simple strength of character, a powerful commitment to basic values that would allow them to make sharp distinctions between good and evil and to steer a virtuous course through a world that had many temptations and few sources of moral support and stability.

To teach these simple values, mothers turned to a vast new literature written explicitly for children. Formal moral instruction in the home consisted most often of mothers reading to children from such popular books as T.H. Gallaudet's *Child's Book of the Soul*, Lydia Sigourney's *The Boys Book*, or the celebrated stories of Peter Parley (Samuel G. Goodrich). Combined with Bible-reading and Sunday-school tracts, these works provided a rich curriculum for the early moral education of nineteenth-century children.[12]

Mothers focused almost exclusively on moral training, giving little attention to intellectual instruction. Sharing a widespread nineteenth-century view, they feared that precocious intellectual activity could both damage physical health and warp emotional and spiritual development. If children happened to learn the rudiments of reading or even the alphabet, that was likely a by-product rather than the object of maternal instruction. Literacy had not lost its importance—indeed, the ability to read the moralistic literature of the day was thought to be essential in keeping alive the lessons of childhood—but parents were increasingly willing to entrust reading instruction to the schools when children were at a more appropriate age for intellectual activity.[13]

Moral Education and the Growth of Schools

Although the role of the mother in moral education was always primary in the nineteenth century, Americans never placed the entire burden on her shoulders. They expected schools—both Sunday schools and daily schools—to extend and reinforce the moral education of the home as they taught children elementary skills of literacy and numeracy. Indeed, the growing importance of formal educational institutions for the young in the period after the Revolution may be attributed in large part to the need for agencies that could offer intensive training during the critical formative years.

The Sunday School

The emergence of the Sunday School was one important indication of the quest for formal agencies to assist parents in the task of moral education. Imported from England in the 1790s, the Sunday school initially served as an agency to instruct poor children in eastern cities, teaching them reading and writing as well moral values. Under the influence of a wave of evangelicalism in the early decades of the nineteenth century, however, it came to focus more narrowly on moral education and to open its doors to children of all backgrounds. In this form it became popular among Protestants of all social classes and grew rapidly across the country, in rural areas as well as in cities.[14]

The Creation of the Public School

As much as Protestant Americans of the nineteenth century valued the Sunday school, they never believed that it could serve as more than an adjunct in the task of moral education. One day a week was simply too little time to give to a process that required constant and intensive effort. Thus, it was to the common daily school that Americans turned to find primary support for the early educational efforts of the family.

Colonial Americans had supported schools only sporadically, giving to them a somewhat marginal place in the education of the masses of children. After the Revolution, however, enrollments increased dramatically, and the school acquired a distinct and important place in an increasingly standardized pattern of moral education. By the early 1830s, it was common in the northern and middle states for parents to provide an intensive early moral education, then to send their young to schools for three or four years sometime between the ages of five and twelve.[15]

Before the 1830s, parents sent their children to a hodgepodge of denominational, charity, and private schools. Between 1830 and 1860, however, Americans began to construct a vast new system of public schools that would quickly become the most important educational institutions of the nineteenth century. Public schools were either low-fee or no-fee schools designed specifically to be open to all white children on a roughly equal basis. By making education universal, Americans hoped to spread a common culture, to plant internal restraints in children of all backgrounds, and to provide a certain minimum level of equal opportunity in the society.

Although the public school won broad support from all social groups, leadership for the movement for publicly financed schools came from the upper and middle classes. More than others, these groups feared the consequences of democratization and economic freedom, and they hoped to use the school as a way to promote order and harmony in an age when instability seemed to be an ever-present threat. They were worried not just about the character of their own children but also about the moral education of other people's children, especially the children of America's rapidly growing immigrant population.

Deeply concerned that liberty could turn into anarchy, leaders of the movement to create public schools sought to use moral education for more than the achievement of personal salvation; they saw the widespread diffusion of moral education to all groups in the society as a way to preserve harmony and order. They often feared and distrusted the families of the poor and the immigrants, not to mention blacks and Native Americans, and they hoped to use the public school, even where it was racially segregated, as an institution for remedial moral instruction. Their hope was that the children of the "dangerous classes" would be lured into the public school by the opportunity for a free elementary education, but if that did not work, they were ready to support compulsory education laws. What was critical was that *all* children learn self-restraint through a common moral code.[16]

Crucible of Character:
The Public School Classroom

Although the public school softened denominational influences on education, it emphasized moral training every bit as much as the most sectarian of private schools. Even when nineteenth-century Americans defined the goals of public schooling in political or economic terms, they invariably accepted moral education as the proper means to achieve their ends. In this society so free of institutional restraints, moral training seemed equally important to the creation of the diligent worker, the responsible citizen, and the man or woman of virtue. The centrality of moral education remained an article of faith from the creation of the public school system in the 1830s until the last decade of the century.

The Preference for Women Teachers

Nothing revealed the importance of moral education in the public school so clearly as the overwhelming preference for women teachers. Women were the acknowledged experts in moral training in the nineteenth century, and most Americans insisted that, when possible, they teach the early grades of public schooling. "A great part already, and it is hoped that a greater part hereafter, of the business of instruction in schools," declared Boston educator George B. Emerson, "must be performed by females.

Everything indicated the natural adaptation of the female character to this vocation."[17]

Across the country, churches, missionary societies, and organizations of reformers enlisted women in a vast crusade to provide the school with proper teachers. One group alone, the National Board of Popular Education, sent nearly six hundred single women to the West to insure that children in these newly settled territories had access to a proper Christian culture. Other groups sponsored a similar foray into the South as a part of the effort to reconstruct that region after the Civil War.[18]

What qualified particular women for teaching positions was their character and reputation rather than any special training or even their general level of education. Although school leaders constantly tried to upgrade the pedagogical skills of teachers, even tough-minded reformers were willing to forgive a woman "her ignorance of syntax and low level of scholarship" if she had "common sense and a good heart."[19]

The primary task of the female teacher in the classroom was to exercise a strong moral influence on the child, reinforcing the lessons of the mother both by serving as a model and by eliciting proper behavior from the child. The stakes were widely acknowledged to be high. "Instructors not only form a character for this world and one that will be estimated by men," wrote one educator, "but likewise a character for eternity, and one that will be estimated by a holy and righteous God."[20] Like the mother herself, the teacher of the nineteenth century carried a heavy burden of moral responsibility.

As models, teachers were expected to exhibit virtue both in and outside the classroom. Always subject to a severe public scrutiny, they had little privacy and virtually no latitude for mistakes in moral judgment. They were almost invariably single, widowed, or older women with grown children, since younger married women were generally expected to confine their work to the home. In many communities, teachers boarded with various respectable families, both as a way to save their spare earnings and to protect their reputations.

In the daily routines of the classroom, teachers paid special attention to the behavior of their children, carefully encouraging good habits and punishing bad ones. Here their efforts were heavily informed by the faculty psychology so popular from the 1820s to the 1890s. That psychology viewed the human mind as a collection of certain faculties and tendencies (moral and emotional as well as intellectual) that could be strengthened by exercise. Following the logic of faculty psychology, teachers worked hard to elicit and reward self-restraint, industry, honesty, kindness, punctuality, and orderliness and to discourage slovenliness, inattention, dishonesty, and unkindness.

In shaping the behavior of their students, teachers were far more likely to depend on gentle encouragement than on harsh penalties. Although the rod was hardly unknown in classrooms of the day, teachers resorted to it only when other approaches failed. The aim of their classroom activities was not to preserve an orderly learning environment but rather to win student assent to certain values, to cultivate in the young minds a love of virtue, and to develop moral commitments that would last a lifetime. To impose severe external restraints in the classroom was hardly an adequate preparation for a life in which virtuous behavior was seen as the product of powerful internal controls.

The Textbook: Repository of Truth

The task of guiding the behavior of children required of teachers an extraordinary combination of skill, persistence, patience, and understanding. Academic instruction, however, depended less on the efforts of the teacher than on textbooks, which occupied a place of central importance in the nineteenth-century classroom. What gave textbooks such preeminence was the sense that they conveyed simply and forcefully the universal truths that underlay morality. Such truths required little explanation and few glosses. If teachers could assure that textbooks were read, the texts themselves would provide the proper moral instruction.

Moral lessons suffused nineteenth-century textbooks—not just readers but spellers and arithmetic books as well. Early exercises emphasized "carefully chosen maxims and selections" meant to be "committed to memory and deeply engraved by frequent repetition." More advanced students learned of the alluring disguises of temptation and the dangers of straying from the paths of virtue by reading ever more complicated "stories selected for the lesson they teach and talked over in such a way to develop the moral judgment in applying familiar principles."[21]

The values themselves were a blend of traditional Protestant morality and nineteenth-century conceptions of good citizenship. Textbooks taught "love of country, love of God, duty to parents, the necessity to develop habits of thrift, honesty, and hard work in order to accumulate property, the certainty of progress [and] the perfection of the United States."[22] Famous spellers and readers, like those of Noah Webster and William Holmes McGuffey, warned ominously of the dangers of drunkenness, luxury, self-pride, and deception and promised handsome earthly rewards for courage, honesty, and respect for others.

A story in McGuffey's *Third Eclectic Reader* was typical of the genre. It told the tale of two boys, Charlie and Rob, who discussed their futures while performing their chore of chopping wood. Charlie hated the task and sought to find easier ways to the riches he dreamed of. Rob, on the other hand, learned from the challenge and worked at other laborious tasks as well. He was not averse to the idea of becoming rich himself, but he did not intend to shirk his duties in the meantime, even if Charlie chose to laugh at him. The moral became clear in the rhetorical question that brought the story to an end: "Now which of these boys, do you think, grew up to be a rich and useful man, and which of them joined a party of tramps before he was thirty?"[23]

Morality, Self-Restraint, and Good Citizenship

Although the values in this and other popular schoolbooks had been familiar for generations, nineteenth-century Americans gave them a peculiarly rigid quality. Fearful that the absence of external restraints would allow a single deviation to grow unchecked into a pattern of wickedness, they painted good and evil in stark, absolute terms and left no gray areas in their moral education—no room for interpretation, no flexibility to apply values as shifting contingencies might dictate. They believed that only absolute rules rigidly adhered to could provide a reliable guide to behavior and protect against the enormous temptations of the day.

From a modern perspective, the early moral education of a nineteenth-century child may be characterized as an effort to create what David Riesman has labelled "the inner-directed man," that is a person who when confronted with a moral dilemma is less guided by tradition or the opinion of others than by values internalized at an early age.[24] In Freudian terms, nineteenth-century moral education created powerful superegos that almost reflexively recoiled from familiar temptation. In the language of the nineteenth-century Americans themselves, the effort was to develop powerful consciences. As educator Horace Mann put it, the goal of moral education was to

> build up a partition wall—a barrier—so thick and high, between the principles of right and wrong, in the minds of men, that the future citizens will not overleap or break through it. A truly conscientious man, whatever may be his desire, his temptation, his appetite, the moment he approaches the boundary line which separates right from wrong, beholds an obstruction—a barrier—more impassable than a Chinese wall. He could sooner leap the ocean, than transgress it.[25]

Moral education so pervaded the classrooms of elementary schools in the nineteenth century that there was little time for instruction in government or politics. Textbooks of the day encouraged patriotism and obedience to the law but gave remarkably little attention to national heroes or political traditions. When the names of prominent statesmen were evoked, the aim was more often to illuminate a moral truth than to exalt the nation's history. Thus, George Washington came to be better known for his honesty than for his political or military skill.

The neglect of government and politics was far from a sign of nonchalance about citizenship, however. Rather, it reflected the peculiar nineteenth-century conception of good citizenship. Americans of that day believed that the key to the good of the society lay less in structures of government or in political beliefs than in the morality of common citizens. In a land of liberty, a land of relatively weak governmental structures, the morality of the individual citizen held out the best hope for the preservation of freedom, the protection of order, and the growth of prosperity. As one educator told an audience of western academicians in 1837: "Sceptered hands, a powerful aristocracy, military force, an omnipresent police—these are the means of preserving peace and order among other nations of the earth. But here they have no place. We are necessarily self-governed, and therefore the absence of these external physical restraints must be supplied by a universal infusion of moral principles."[26]

This nineteenth-century tendency to place personal moral conduct at the core of their hopes for social stability and political liberty gave to the elementary school a significance it had never had before. Not only did parents send their children to the schools in unprecedented numbers, but taxpayers paid handsome sums with surprisingly little dissent to support public schools that gradually eliminated tuition fees and made elementary education widely accessible to children of all social stations.

Beyond the Early Years

Given common assumptions about the importance of early moral education, it is no surprise that elementary schools constituted the core of the public school system. By the Civil War 85 to 90 percent of children between the ages of seven and thirteen in the state of Massachusetts were enrolled in school, and enrollment rates in many other states approached those rates.[27] The overwhelming majority of these children were in elementary schools. Although precise statistics are not available, probably no more than 10 percent of the eligible population attended academies, high schools, or colleges. Nor, in fact, did Americans attribute great political or cultural significance to advanced education. In an age when the character was thought to be shaped in the early years, elementary schools were the primary beneficiaries of public support for education.

The conviction that elementary schools played the essential role in moral education freed secondary schools and colleges to offer a broader and more utilitarian curriculum than they had in the eighteenth century. Americans increasingly associated education at these levels with occupational and social success rather than with cultural coherence or political stability. Yet even a society that believed in the early formation of character did not relieve these higher educational institutions entirely of responsibility for moral education. Like other institutions in the society, they were influenced by the waves of Protestant evangelicalism, piety, and moralism that were so central to nineteenth-century American society, and they were expected to exercise a careful supervision over the behavior of their students, thereby systematically reinforcing the moral lessons of childhood.

The work of academies and high schools in the nineteenth century varied enormously. Some institutions offered curricula little different from the colleges, others continued slightly modified versions of the classical studies of the Latin grammar school, and still others—a growing number as the century progressed—offered a broad range of courses, including some decidedly utilitarian subjects. Elite academies, like the colleges they competed with, sometimes included courses in ethics and moral philosophy, but most secondary institutions provided no formal moral training. If textbooks continued to reflect the familiar values, they did so in a less insistent way. Character, of course, was a matter of concern for educators at every level, but the daily routines of secondary schools focused primarily on the practical tasks of preparing its students for college or a career. Secondary schools rarely provided systematic religious instruction, even of a nondenominational sort, except where private institutions were sponsored by churches.[28]

Colleges were more often tied to specific religious denominations, especially in the first half of the nineteenth century, and they continued to offer formal religious and moral instruction. Although some of the great colonial colleges had drifted away from orthodoxy, many of the newly founded institutions of the day had been created specifically to promote the cause of one sect or another and to provide it with ministers, missionaries, and a measure of status. Reversing the secular drift of eighteenth-century colleges, these institutions injected a heavy dose of piety back into higher education, bringing it into line with the evangelistic and moralistic tenor of the times.[29]

Moral education appeared in a variety of places in the college curriculum, but formal instruction was most systematic in the course in moral philosophy, a virtually universal offering in the nineteenth-century colleges. Moral philosophy was often the capstone course in the curriculum, and the men who taught it (including some college presidents) occupied a place of unique standing among nineteenth-century academics.

During the antebellum years courses in moral philosophy were re-markably comprehensive offerings that sought to bring Christian ethics to bear on an array of personal and social matters ranging from proper fam-ily relationships to issues in criminal justice. Heavily influenced by Scot-tish common-sense realism, moral philosophers of the day posited the existence of a moral sense accessible to all people and emphasized the duty of individuals to adhere to basic moral principles. Unlike their predeces-sors of the Enlightenment era, they gave relatively little attention to the role of prudence in moral decision-making, virtually ignoring the calcula-tion of consequences as a part of the moral act. Instead they emphasized the importance of intention and reinforced the popular tendency to view morality as a matter of bringing the will into conformity with absolute and universal moral rules.[30]

By embracing Scottish common-sense realism, American moral phi-losophers gave intellectual authority to the two primary thrusts in ante-bellum culture—the quest for liberty in economic and political realms and the emphasis on restraint and inner controls in morality. Little in their teach-ing gave students a critical perspective from which they might have chal-lenged the classical liberal state or softened the rigid morality of the day. When students sought access to other intellectual traditions, they had to go beyond the usual offerings of the classroom, often buying their own books and even creating their own student-run libraries which could be fully stocked with Enlightenment texts.

Occasional student protest notwithstanding, colleges attempted to reinforce the formal instruction of the moral philosophy courses with a carefully controlled extracurricular life. College builders deliberately chose small-town locations as a way to protect students from the lures of big cit-ies and often housed students in dormitories where their behavior could be closely supervised. Members of the faculty attended to the moral de-velopment of their charges as much as to their intellectual growth. If stu-dents sometimes revolted against this piety, as they did when they formed literary societies or social fraternities, they were also capable of reinforc-ing it, as the countless campus religious revivals of the day attest.[31]

Although both secondary schools and colleges offered some opportu-nity for dissent, or at least nonconcern, the antebellum era was remark-able for the extent to which a uniform approach to morality prevailed up and down the largely Protestant educational ladder. In the eighteenth cen-tury, colleges had often been hostile to orthodoxy and had sometimes en-couraged students to reexamine cherished beliefs. This would be the case again in the late nineteenth century when science began to raise new ques-tions about conventional beliefs, but in the antebellum years, the college experience only reenforced the basic values that children had first learned at their mothers' knees.

Consensus and Conflict

The congruity of moral philosophy with common conceptions of morality gave a strong sense of certainty about moral questions to many Americans. Uniformity across the levels of education, however, fell far short of reflecting a consensus on either the form or content of moral education, for despite the universalistic goals of many educational leaders, both public schools and antebellum colleges were primarily Protestant institutions in a society with a small but growing Catholic population. Catholics and Protestants had wide areas of agreement on what constituted a proper moral education, but they differed sharply on a critical issue, namely the place of religion in moral instruction. In an age when virtually everyone believed that morality should be rooted in faith, differences with regard to the place of religion were inevitably divisive, and in the antebellum era the differences created one of the fiercest and most enduring conflicts in American history. It is this conflict and other disputes about the place of religion in moral education that constitute the subject of the next chapter.

CHAPTER THREE

Religion and Moral Education: American Configurations

As Americans of the nineteenth century grappled with the problem of moral education, they made a fateful decision about schools. Instead of following the path of most European countries and building on a long tradition of state support for religious education, they undertook the construction of a vast new system of nonsectarian public schooling. The aim was not to forbid religion in the classroom but rather to teach a nonsectarian Christianity at public expense, leaving to other institutions the responsibility for instruction in the fine points of theological doctrine. A response to the diversity of the society, nonsectarian schooling was an effort to find a common ground in moral education, thereby enhancing cohesion while protecting the rights of particular denominations to preserve their special doctrinal truths.

The movement to establish nonsectarian schooling had its roots in a variety of religious, cultural, and political impulses of the early nineteenth century. From the first, it was a thoroughly Protestant campaign. It drew heavily on Protestant social thought and Protestant modes of organization, and it recruited a disproportionate number of its leaders from the Protestant clergy. Moved at first by their own internal divisions and later by fears of a growing Catholic presence, Protestants saw in public education a chance to put the stamp of their own values on the entire society.

This quest for Protestant hegemony drew strength from a more generalized fear of disorder and faction in the first half of the nineteenth century. The social and political disruptions that accompanied democratization, the westward movement, and the breakdown of the family economy provided a background of anxiety against which the quest for a nonsectarian schooling took place. The same forces that led families to develop new concerns about the moral well-being of their children in these years led communities to rally to the support of a nonsectarian public schooling that would serve as a common meeting ground for all white children regardless of background. The public school would be, in the words of Horace

Mann, "one institution, at least, which shall be spared from the ravages of the spirit of party, one spot in the wide land unblasted by the fiery breath of animosity . . . one rallying-point for a peaceful and harmonious co-operation and fellowship."[1]

The Roots of Nonsectarianism
in American Life

The notion that nonsectarianism offered hope for both the spread of the Christian faith and the achievement of social harmony was forged during the Second Great Awakening, the series of religious revivals that swept across the country in the early decades of the nineteenth century. These revivals produced paradoxical results. On the one hand, they created divisions within many traditional denominations, furthering a process of splintering that had long been a part of Protestantism. On the other hand, they tended to soften the lines between sects by emphasizing a religion of the heart that devalued formal creeds and weakened the hold of orthodoxies. Moreover, they encouraged the creation of a network of nondenominational societies designed to hasten the spread of the gospel and give new energy to the work of Christian mission. Thus, such groups as the American Bible Society and the American Home Missionary Society brought together evangelical Protestants from a wide range of denominations in an effort to spread revival and Christian nurture across the land. Eventually the soldiers in these various crusades began to think of themselves not simply as Presbyterians or Methodists but also as a part of a great pan-Protestant moral empire, an empire they found it increasingly easy to identify with America itself.[2]

The interdenominational approach to religious revival that developed during the Second Great Awakening became a widely copied model for a whole array of moral and social reform movements during the years before the Civil War. Whether they were campaigning against slavery or for temperance, reformers of the early and mid-nineteenth century worked less through their particular church denominations or political parties than through broad nonsectarian societies. Like the evangelicals, they believed that success required them to subordinate their doctrinal differences in the interest of spreading common truths, achieving reform, and promoting social harmony.

Although the bias toward nonsectarianism exhibited in these moral crusades was never universal among Protestants, the idea had a powerful influence among a substantial majority, and its hold on the culture grew throughout the century. In important respects nonsectarianism was an early form of American pluralism, and it operated in the daily life of communities as well as in the great religious and reform movements of the day. In towns and neighborhoods where relatively homogeneous religious communities had been split by the revivals of the Second Great Awakening, nonsectarianism allowed Americans to sustain a level of social cohesion even as they nourished a measure of religious diversity. In their public activities, men and women emphasized their commitment to the common tenets of Christian faith; in the more private spheres of family and church, they continued to confess their particular versions of religious doctrine. Thus, where communities were divided on such theological issues as original sin or infant baptism, they were careful to muffle the public expression of their differences and to proclaim instead their common faith in the ten commandments, the golden rule, and the redemptive power of Jesus Christ.

It was out of this culture that nineteenth-century Americans gradually shaped an approach to moral education that was meant both to create a strong consensus on Christian values and to preserve the rights of individuals to hold to their particular sectarian doctrines. The public school was to be the primary expression of this approach, but a transformed Sunday school was also an integral part of the scheme. Viewed broadly, the goal of reformers was to teach children universal moral values and a generalized Protestant religion in the public school while reserving to the home and the Sunday school the task of inculcating the special doctrines of their particular faiths.

The Complementary Roles of Public Schools and Sunday Schools

The fundamental premise of this approach was that moral education could be rooted in a generalized set of Christian values without aggravating sectarian differences. "There are," declared Heman Humphrey, the president of Amherst College and one of the great champions of nonsectarian schooling, "certain moral and religious principles, in which all denominations are agreed, such as the Ten Commandments, our Saviour's Golden Rule, everything, in short, which lies within the whole range of duty to God and duty to our fellow man."[3] The task of the school was simply to teach these Christian truths without involving itself in specific doctrinal disputes. "Let the grown people be trinitarians and unitarians, Catholics and Protestants," exhorted one reformer, "be content to let the children be Christians."[4]

The linchpin of this nonsectarian strategy was the practice of reading the Bible in schools without offering any interpretation or gloss. To read the Bible without comment was to invoke an authority that no Protestant could dispute, without at the same time taking a stand on any of the issues that set denominations against one another. As Heman Humphrey put it, the advantage of Bible-reading over other forms of religious instruction was "that every denomination believes so far as it differs from the rest that the Bible is on its side, and, of course, the more it is read by all the better." To object to Bible-reading was "to confess that I had not full confidence in my own creed and was afraid it would not bear a scriptural test."[5]

The presence of the Bible in the schools became a powerful symbol of the connections between religion and morality, and Protestants resisted any effort to remove it. Moreover, where denominational sensitivities allowed, public school educators also encouraged prayer, hymn-singing, and other religious exercises. Yet despite the presence of religion, most moral education focused on values that required little theological sanction, values such as honesty, industry, thrift, and kindness. Because the aim was to heal divisions and subordinate differences, the public school inevitably emphasized those parts of the culture that enjoyed the support of a broad (albeit mainly Protestant) consensus and avoided issues that divided one sect or party from another.

As public schools came to be the primary institutional custodians of nonsectarian approaches to moral education, the Sunday school moved in precisely the opposite direction, abandoning the broad interdenominational effort to bring Christian discipline and discipleship to the working classes and becoming instead an adjunct to particular churches, serving as the vehicle through which the special doctrinal truths of the denominations were passed along to children. With public schools increasingly teaching literacy and morality to children of all social stations, Sunday schools were free to offer an explicitly religious education, one that emphasized the very doctrines that were forbidden in state-supported institutions.[6]

Most Protestants clearly understood the roles of the public school and the Sunday school to be complementary. Together, these two institutions seemed to offer an ideal way to preserve social harmony while nurturing at least a narrow range of religious diversity. Characteristically, the scheme allowed Americans to emphasize their commonness in the public setting of the nonsectarian school while confining their doctrinal differences to the relatively private spheres of church and home.

Not all Protestants, to be sure, were comfortable with this particular division of labor in moral education. Some pietistic sects spurned formal education altogether, and others insisted on educating children in their own carefully supervised schools. Even some mainline Protestants were initially skeptical of nonsectarian schools. By the middle of the century, however, the vast majority of Protestants had accepted the new arrangement, content to separate the general moral education offered in the public school from the religious training provided by family, church, and Sunday school.

Catholicism and the Public School

The Catholic "Problem"

The combination of nonsectarian public schooling and denominational Sunday schooling was in many respects an ingenious solution to the problem of religious diversity among Protestants. Yet at the same time that many Americans thought that they had resolved the problems of moral education in a religiously diverse society, a growing Catholic population created a new challenge, one that could not be met by simply applying the Protestant scheme to a wider group of actors.

Many of the earliest public school supporters apparently gave little thought to the challenge presented by the Catholic presence. Obsessed by the need to shore up Protestant unity and mission, they made no provision to accommodate the then relatively small Catholic population. Other reformers were more sensitive, however, and their concern became widespread in the 1840s and 1850s as the Catholic population began a period of explosive growth. By mid-century, neither educational leaders nor public school supporters could ignore the matter, and a range of responses emerged.

The most generous of school reformers, such as Horace Mann, hoped to attract Catholics to the public school. Their vision of social cohesion required that all children regardless of background should be schooled in common values, and they pressed to make the public school a broadly inclusive institution. To exclude Catholics, they feared, was not simply to aggravate sectarian hostilities but also to alienate the working class and immigrants, many of whom were Catholic. To exclude workers and immigrants was to weaken the school's power to serve as a cohesive force in the society and to increase the prospect that the children of the "dangerous classes" would grow up undisciplined, illiterate, and a threat to the stability of the society. "It is," declared Cincinnati educator Calvin E. Stowe, "no longer a mere question of benevolence, of duty, or of enlightened self-interest, but the intellectual and religious training of our foreign population has become essential to our own safety; we are prompted to it by the instinct of self-preservation."[7]

These reformers, even when they harbored anti-Catholic and anti-immigrant feelings of their own, sought to soften the nativist impulses in the public school movement and to make compromises that would attract

Catholics to the schools. Horace Mann, for example, admonished his Protestant supporters that teaching creeds offensive to immigrants might result in excluding more than half of the children of Boston from the schools. Reformers in Ohio joined with immigrants to secure legislation that allowed public schools in German districts to teach the native language as well as English. A few educators even took the extraordinary step of suggesting that both Catholic (Douay) and Protestant (King James) translations of the Bible be read in the classroom.[8] In proposing such compromises, these reformers often went beyond their more cautious colleagues and far beyond many of their constituents, who were unwilling to accept immigrants and Catholics into public schools on anything other than strict assimilationist terms. In fact, some natives were not enthusiastic about attracting these outsiders at all. Instead, they viewed public education as a way for their children to maintain a differential advantage over immigrants and resisted reformist schemes that might bring their potential competitors into the school. The need of these natives for status and material gain simply outweighed their commitment to commonality and cohesion, and their opposition did much to thwart the effort of reformers who sought to make the public school an inclusive institution.

Disagreements among Protestants on the Catholic issue were reflected in actual educational practice. In a few places educators made accommodations, employing some Catholic teachers, allowing Scripture reading from the Douay version of the Bible, and screening textbooks for material offensive to Catholics. More often, however, schools exhibited an unyielding commitment to Protestant practices. Many common textbooks of the day were virulently anti-Catholic, and many others contained subtle condemnations of both immigrants and Catholics. Teachers continued to read primarily from the King James version of the Bible, and religious exercises in the schools retained a distinctly Protestant cast. Only in a few scattered cities and towns could nineteenth-century Catholics have found anything but hostility and insensitivity in the public schools.

Catholic Traditions in Moral Education

Initial Catholic criticism of nonsectarian public schooling focused on the most obvious and offensive abuses, a fact that led some Protestant educators to underestimate just how fundamental Catholic opposition to nonsectarian moral education really was. In fact, Catholics found the notion of nonsectarian moral education deeply at odds with their own doctrines and traditions, and even a cleaning up of offensive Protestant textbooks would not likely have made the public school an appealing place for them.

As F. Michael Perko has pointed out, nineteenth-century Catholicism was a deeply traditional religion with fundamental presuppositions that were radically different from the Protestant worldview. Unlike Protestants, Catholics associated individual salvation less with personal conversion or upright behavior than with participation in the rich sacramental life of the church. Moreover, they were reluctant to confine the authority of the church to narrow spheres, to separate the sacred from the civil, to draw lines between public and private domains, or to make sharp distinctions between universally acceptable truths and the doctrinal beliefs of particular denominations.[9]

In the realm of education, most Catholics ascribed primary responsibility to the family and the church and were reluctant to acknowledge an autonomous role for the state, preferring instead a scheme that would give public support for private educational efforts. They criticized the public school because it seemed to them only a faintly disguised Protestant enterprise, yet were never able to envision clearly an alternative approach to nonsectarian schooling that would satisfy their own needs. The habit of connecting moral education to their specific tradition was simply too ingrained. Unlike Protestants who had devalued doctrine as they advocated a religion of the heart, Catholics continued to emphasize the catechism as the beginning point for moral education, and they found it difficult to imagine a schooling devoid of elementary doctrinal instruction.

Bible-reading offered no way out of this dilemma for Catholics. They were accustomed to studying the Scriptures only in light of other teachings of the church, and the Protestant habit of letting the Bible speak for itself was entirely alien to their tradition. In their view, Scripture-reading unaccompanied by other instruction revealed only partial truths. Thus, even the use of the Douay Bible in the public school classroom, while an encouraging sign of Protestant tolerance, was not enough to meet the highest Catholic standards for the integration of moral and religious education.

The Failure of Compromise

Despite the profound differences in their traditions, Catholics and Protestants of the nineteenth and twentieth centuries made repeated and frequently heroic attempts to compromise on the question of moral education. Some public school leaders were willing to allow the reading of the Douay Bible or even to release students for private religious instruction in order to lure Catholics into the schools. Many Catholic families for their part sent their children to public schools, often in defiance of church authorities, and a number of Catholic clergy sought to create schemes that would have allowed Catholic religious instruction within a publicly controlled and financed system.

Such efforts at compromise produced many local successes. In the 1830s, for example, the public school system of Lowell, Massachusetts incorporated two previously Catholic schools with the understanding that it would continue to employ Catholic teachers and exclude textbooks offensive to Catholics. In this case, the school board had full authority to inspect and control schools, hire teachers, and determine curriculum; it succeeded in retaining Catholic support because it used its authority to protect diversity rather than to impose a single approach to moral education across the system.[10] In other cities, the option of using the Douay translation of the Bible was enough to attract Catholic children, at least for a short time.

Accommodations of this sort, though frequent throughout the nineteenth and even the twentieth century, never pointed to a general resolution of the differences between Catholics and Protestants on the question of moral education. Not only were fundamental religious and ideological differences great, they were complicated by nativism among certain Protestants and by the efforts of ethnic Catholics to use education as a way of preserving the cultures of their homelands. If some people on both sides continued to seek common ground, many others insisted on a schooling that reflected their particular traditions. In the end, difference triumphed and American education became divided between a public system that offered a nonsectarian schooling to the vast majority of children and several parochial systems that continued to combine religion and moral education in ways that particular denominations demanded. Of these parochial systems, the Catholic was by far the largest.

Origins of the Catholic Parochial System

Sharp differences between Catholics and Protestants emerged soon after the campaign for nonsectarian schooling scored its impressive early gains. Tensions erupted first in New York in the early 1840s. There Bishop John Hughes of New York City sought public funds to support Catholic schools, arguing that moneys distributed by the New York Public School Society effectively supported Protestant schools. Although Hughes was able to win the support of Governor William H. Seward, alarmed Protestants persuaded the state legislature to restrict aid to nonsectarian schools. Since the legislature subsequently authorized Bible-reading in the classroom, the state had effectively elevated the Protestant approach to moral education into public policy. Hughes responded by encouraging Catholic parishes to create their own schools and Catholic parents to provide a specifically Catholic education for their children.

Similar public policy in Pennsylvania evoked an even sharper response and led to a violent confrontation between Catholics and Protestants. Operating under an 1838 law that required that the Scriptures be used in the teaching of reading, Philadelphia schools in 1842 fired a teacher for refusing to read from the King James Bible and spanked a child for the same offense. After Catholic protests, the school board made some symbolic compromises (allowing children to read from preferred translations "without notes or comments"—a phrase that technically eliminated the Douay version, which included commentary). Nativists, however, were in no mood to compromise, even symbolically, and they began to march through Catholic districts of the city in protest during the summer of 1844. The result was a series of violent confrontations that resulted in hundreds of casualties, including more than forty deaths. Only the use of troops finally curtailed the fighting.[11]

The events of New York and Philadelphia were enough to sober early Catholic hopes for some accommodation with the public school. Moreover, they were followed by a decade and a half of increasingly vicious nativism that hardened positions on both sides of the debate about religion and education. By the late 1840s, a growing number of Catholics had despaired of finding a place within a publicly financed system of schooling. Gradually a variety of local initiatives to create parochial schools coalesced into a broad national effort to fashion a distinct Catholic system of education.

The national scope of the movement to create a Catholic system became evident at the First Plenary Council of Baltimore in 1852. Here, bishops from across the United States resolved that parishes should create their own schools. Perhaps still nourishing the hope for state aid, the bishops left hanging the question of how such schools should be financed but urged the parishes themselves to assume final responsibility for support of the system.

What was purely voluntary after the decrees of the First Plenary Council became mandatory during the Third Plenary Council of Baltimore in 1884. This national gathering of American bishops ordered all parishes to establish schools within two years and outlined penalties for priests and congregations who failed to do so without adequate cause. Moreover, it decreed "that all Catholic parents are bound to send their children to the parish school, unless it is evident that a sufficient training in religion is given either in their own homes, or in other Catholic schools; or when because of a sufficient reason, approved by the bishop, with all due precautions and safeguards, it is licit to send them to other schools."[12]

By the end of the nineteenth century the Catholic school system was firmly entrenched in virtually every part of the country, and it was clear to even the most ardent public school leaders that the grand vision of a single system of nonsectarian education was as far away as ever. The creation of the parochial school, however, did not forever resolve the questions that divided Protestants and Catholics on education. Burdened by an expensive private system, some Catholics continued to seek financial support from the state, focusing at first on accommodations with local public schools and then, in the mid-twentieth century, launching a quest for federal aid.

At the local level, some Catholics found it possible to put aside the goal of a purely parochial education and thereby to win financial support for schools that continued to offer religious education. In 1873, for example, a Poughkeepsie, New York parish invited the public school board to assume substantial control over two former parochial schools. The school board paid the costs of instruction and selected teachers and textbooks with the approval of the pastor. The church provided religious education before and after school and controlled the physical facilities when they were not being used for classes.

The Poughkeepsie plan was copied in several cities in New York and New England, and a similar scheme in Faribault, Minnesota had at least a short-lived influence in the Midwest. In general, eastern Catholics were more enthusiastic about these plans than were westerners, but nowhere did such accommodations become more than purely local arrangements, the product less of clear public policy than of pockets of tolerance in a land where lines between public and private education were being defined in increasingly severe terms.

The quest for federal aid was even less successful. Catholics began their efforts to win federal support after the Second World War, when public schools were also looking to Washington for help. In order to avoid inflaming the church-state issue, Catholics focused their efforts on obtaining support for auxiliary services such as transportation and health care rather than for instruction. Yet even these modest requests raised fears that Catholics were seeking public support for the total programs of their schools. Although court decisions did not forbid aid to auxiliary services, a powerful coalition of Protestants, Jews, and liberal secularists effectively blocked every significant Catholic effort to obtain federal support.

Despite these failures to win state financial support, Catholic parochial education continued to show a remarkable vitality. The peak of enrollment came in the mid-1960s when 5.6 million students attended Catholic elementary and secondary schools. For a variety of reasons, including the burden of double taxation on Catholic parents, enrollment has declined steadily since 1965. By 1989, enrollment had decreased to 2,551,119.[13] Nevertheless, the Catholic parochial school system remained the nation's largest system of private education, offering a significant alternative to the public school.

Other Dissenting Traditions

From the beginning of the public school movement, Catholics formed the largest group of dissenters, and the parochial school system they erected in the last half of the nineteenth century remains to this day an important barrier to the ancient dream of a single system of public schooling. Yet Catholics have hardly been the only critics of the nonsectarian school. Several Protestant denominations have also either rejected the public school or made uneasy accommodations with it. Likewise, Jews and Eastern Orthodox groups, while usually willing to send their children to the public school, have often found it necessary to counter its Protestant bias with after-hours or Sunday school instruction in the tenets of their own particular faiths.

Of the Protestant dissenters, the most powerful have come from the Lutheran tradition. Many Lutherans, to be sure, rallied to the public school relatively early on, though few were among the leaders of the effort to create the system. This was especially the case in the well-settled areas of the East, where most synods abandoned their church schools in the middle decades of the nineteenth century and sent their children instead to the new public schools. A number of synods in the West, however, were far more skeptical of public education, and they elected to create a parochial school system that was not unlike the system created by the Catholic Church.[14]

The strongest and most persistent support for parochial schools came from the Missouri Synod, a conservative synod that actually spanned a number of western states. Overwhelmingly German by background, Missouri Synod Lutherans sought to preserve both their culture and the purity of their religious doctrines by creating schools that would teach German as well as English and would make the catechism an integral part of moral education. Like Catholics, these Lutherans were convinced that a proper moral education required instruction in the specific doctrines of the church; the nonsectarian religion of the public school was simply too vague to provide an adequate basis for preserving the faith or building Christian character.

Missouri Synod Lutherans opened their first parochial schools in the late 1830s. By 1872, they had established 472 schools, which served more than thirty thousand students, roughly one school for every congregation. Growth continued apace throughout the late nineteenth century and began to slow only in the twentieth century, when the creation of new schools began to fall behind the creation of new congregations. Although Missouri Synod schools have become less distinctive over the years (the teaching of German, for example, was abandoned during the First World War), the system has remained strong, enrolling in 1982 more than 177,000 students in 1,584 elementary schools and more than 16,000 students in 61 high schools.[15]

A more diffuse strand of Protestant dissent has emerged only in the twentieth century, but in recent years it has become the major factor in the growth of private religious education. Supported by a range of evangelical and fundamentalist Christians, this movement has produced both a bitter protest against the secularization of public schools and a vigorous effort to create Christian day schools, where religion and morality could once again be taught together. Supported by local congregations or by like-minded Christians from different denominations, Christian day schools have grown dramatically since the mid-1960s, when they began to benefit from both a disillusionment with secular education and, in some parts of the country, from the progress of racial integration in the public schools.[16]

A remarkably diverse group of institutions, Christian day schools have never constituted a system of education. Although some belong to associations of private schools, others are so fiercely independent that they have failed even to report their enrollments. Yet the schools have taken a fairly uniform approach to moral education, rooting it firmly in the Bible and insisting that it infuse every part of school life. As one champion of the scheme has put it, "Christian schools are Christian institutions where Jesus Christ and the Bible are central in the school curriculum and in the lives of teachers and administrators. . . . Ours is a Christ-centered education presented in the Christian context."[17]

Supported by the fastest growing wings of Protestantism, Christian day schools have expanded dramatically in the past quarter century. Given the independence of many of the schools, precise estimates of size and enrollments are difficult to come by, but Bruce S. Cooper and Grace Dondero estimate that in 1989 there were more than seven thousand schools with a total enrollment of more than 985,000 students.[18]

If various Christian denominations have had grounds to find public schools inadequate, Jews have had cause to be even more aggrieved. Nondenominational Christianity may have seemed insubstantial to many Protestants and misguided to Catholics, but to Jews it was entirely outside their religious tradition. Yet Jews have been strong supporters of public education. Seeing it as an avenue to opportunity and respectability in the New World, nineteenth and early twentieth-century Jews, especially those in the Reform tradition, enrolled the vast majority of their children in the public school. At the same time, they made provisions for preserving their religious and cultural traditions, creating Saturday or Sunday Hebrew schools or after-school sessions where children learned Jewish history and religion, often using the same kind of catechetical approaches that Catholics and Lutherans employed in their parochial schools. In some of these schools children learned Hebrew, and after the late nineteenth-century immigration from Eastern Europe, some learned Yiddish as well, which made the Jewish schools a repository for both a religious and a cultural heritage.[19]

Although the majority of Jews sent their children to public schools, a few, especially from Orthodox and Conservative persuasions, favored the Jewish day school, a school that mirrored the Catholic and Lutheran parochial schools by offering both sacred and secular education to its students. Only a small percentage of Jewish children attended the day school during the nineteenth and early twentieth centuries, but beginning in the 1920s the day school entered a period of growth that continued through the middle decades of the century. For reasons that are not entirely clear to historians, day schools became more popular, enrolling more than one hundred thousand students in 1980, as weekend and after-hours programs steadily lost students. Still small by comparative standards, the Jewish day school has nonetheless served as a reminder that some strands of Judaism remain committed to a system that roots moral education firmly in religion.[20]

Education and the Laws
of Church-State Relations

Supporters of public schooling have rarely accepted private religious schools with equanimity. They have worked to prevent public aid to private ventures and have tried on occasion to cripple, even to outlaw, religious schools. In the 1880s and 1890s, for example, Protestant nativists in several states tried to enact laws that would restrict and weaken Catholic and Lutheran parochial schools. In 1889 both Wisconsin and Illinois passed statutes that gave local school boards power to enforce the compulsory attendance of children in schools that were (1) located in districts where they lived and (2) approved schools where English was the language of instruction. Although these statutes did not prevent the use of private institutions to meet the requirements, they were a direct assault on parochial schools, which often offered instruction in German or other immigrant languages and which generally enrolled students from a variety of districts.

Such restrictive legislation rarely succeeded (the Wisconsin and Illinois laws were quickly repealed with devastating political consequences for their supporters), but efforts continued throughout the late nineteenth and early twentieth centuries to retard the growth of private education.

The most extreme measure—and the last significant one—was the Oregon School Law of 1922, which required children between the ages of eight and sixteen to attend public schools. Controversial from the first, the law engendered immediate litigation that ultimately resulted in a Supreme Court decision declaring it unconstitutional.[21]

Although religious schools never again faced the kind of official hostility exhibited in these laws, they also received little encouragement. Public policy remained resolutely opposed to financial aid for church schools, and legal theory and precedent gradually constructed a wall of separation between church and state that was far higher than anything the authors of the Constitution had imagined. During the nineteenth century, it was the state courts interpreting state constitutions that did most to prevent the use of public funds for sectarian schools, but in the twentieth century the federal judiciary, especially the Supreme Court, has taken the lead in blocking efforts to provide state aid to private religious schools.[22]

As courts and legislatures have drawn ever-clearer prohibitions against state aid to private schools, they have found it more difficult to defend the traditional place of Protestant Christianity in public schools. Slowly and often reluctantly, courts began in the late nineteenth century to respond more sympathetically to those who complained about Bible-reading and prayer in the public schools. Especially in the Midwest, where Lutherans, among others, felt strongly about church-state divisions, state courts banned Bible-reading, usually grounding their decisions on state constitutions rather than on federal statutes or precedents. Such decisions did not initially affect practice in many parts of the country, and as late as 1949, twelve states required Bible-reading and twenty-one permitted it. Even in states with clear legal prohibitions, some localities continued to follow traditional practices well into the middle of the century. Only when the Supreme Court declared school prayer illegal in 1962 (*Engel v Vitale*) and Bible-reading illegal in 1963 (*School District of Abington Township, Pennsylvania v Edward Lewis Schemp* 374 U.S. 203) did such religious activities disappear from the public school classroom.

The Ironic Effects of Nonsectarianism

The effort of the Protestant majority in the United States to deal with the problem of religion and moral education by creating a single nonsectarian system of public schooling has produced ironic results. Conceived initially as a system that would create harmony among disparate religious groups, it has instead bred hostility among many of them. From the first, champions of the idea of nonsectarianism underestimated the strength of religious differences in the society, and they failed to find a ground common enough even to unite all Protestants. They did much to spread their own faith, but by trying to turn their particular worldview into a kind of civic religion, they deepened divisions in society, driving embittered dissenters to create their own schools and permanently thwarting the possibility of a single system of public schooling.

Equally ironic has been the connection between nonsectarianism and the secularization of public education. The early Protestant supporters of public schools were insistent on the connections between morality and religion, and they clearly saw the public school as a way to spread the general tenets of Protestant Christianity. Yet in order to prevent state aid to Catholic education, they were compelled to expand the religious neutrality of the public school. With every Catholic charge that public education was effectively Protestant religious education, public school leaders found it necessary to weaken the theological content of moral education. This effort to protect nonsectarianism was not, of course, the only force involved in the secularization of schools, but it clearly was the original source and it accelerated the process from the mid-nineteenth century to the present. By the mid-twentieth century the public school had become so devoid of religious content that even many Protestant groups who had been its strongest defenders now turned against it, finding themselves in the end closer to the Catholic position on religion and morality than to the nonsectarianism that their forebears had done so much to create.

CHAPTER FOUR

The Effects of Modernity, 1890s–1940s

What had been a consensus during most of the nineteenth century among Protestants and Catholics alike, namely, the centrality of moral education in the schools, received its first serious challenge in the last years of the nineteenth century and the early decades of the twentieth. The challenge came not in the form of a frontal assault but stemmed rather from the need of the school to expand its functions in response to the demands of a distinctively modern society. As schools began to teach students the new social, academic, and vocational skills required by a complex corporate and bureaucratic order, moral education was forced to compete for a place in an increasingly crowded curriculum. At the same time, educators began to debate the adequacy of traditional forms of moral training and to explore the possibility that modernity required entirely new approaches to the ancient task of educating moral men and women.

Similar developments began even earlier in institutions of higher education, where the expansion of knowledge and a new sensitivity to professional preparation splintered the curriculum and gave scientific and practical subjects a primacy over cultural and moral studies. Especially in large, prestigious universities, the pursuit of research—both pure and practical—altered the whole tone of the collegiate experience and left educators searching, almost desperately, for ways in which to preserve a place for moral concerns in higher education.

The vast expansion and transformation of education in the late nineteenth and early twentieth centuries represented a response both to changes in the workplace and to new social and cultural forms. The productive system of modern society placed a premium on specialization, technical expertise, and the ability to interact smoothly in an impersonal, rule-governed corporate structure. Success in this system depended less on character in the traditional sense than on skill, efficiency, and social competence. Schools responded by increasing their academic offerings, providing a complex social apprenticing, and offering vocational counseling and instruction. To acquire the new skills, students remained in school for longer and longer periods, as high schools doubled their enrollments in every decade between 1890 and 1940 and colleges began to appeal to a larger and larger clientele.

It was not just the productive side of modern society, however, that led educators to expand and transform the school. Outside the workplace, technological advance and economic abundance created new opportunities for pleasure and recreation at the same time that the growing impersonality of life was freeing individuals from a variety of old restraints. Dance halls, amusement parks, and other forms of mass, commercial recreation grew quickly after the turn of the century, and they were followed in the 1920s by radio and the movies, which carried tantalizing messages of personal freedom to every corner of society. The mass production of the automobile in the late twenties and the growing availability of birth control devices completed the transformation, taking even courtship out of the home and opening up new possibilities for sexual fulfillment. In these circumstances, the worthy use of leisure time as well as new approaches to citizenship became central problems for the modern school, as demanding in their way as were the needs of production.

The dramatic contrasts between the world of work and the world of leisure posed still another problem for modern educators. Once work and leisure had been situated together in the highly personal contexts of neighborhood and community, and a single set of values had served people equally well in every sphere of human endeavor. Now the home, the job, the marketplace, the church, and the place of recreation operated by different rules and rewarded different values. As historian Thomas Bender has put it, "What had been a seamless web of community life broke into segments. . . . Whereas work, family, and town once supplied mutually reenforcing personal orientations, they became crosscutting sources of identity" in the modern world of the twentieth century.[1] Now schools were forced to prepare students for a variety of roles across the differentiated spheres of a segmented social order.

Roots of Reform in Elementary and Secondary Schools

As educators struggled to meet the varied demands of the new order, they gave far more attention to academic achievement and social competence than had their nineteenth-century predecessors. Schools became complex institutions with a variety of purposes, only one of which was moral education. Yet concern for moral education did not disappear. Instead its focus was redirected as Americans raised a new set of questions about the meaning of morality in the context of a rapidly developing modern society.

What emerged from these queries at the level of elementary and secondary education in the first forty years of the twentieth century was not a new conventional wisdom but rather three divergent responses to the problem of moral education in the modern world. Among public educators, two general views contended. One sought to meet the challenges of the new order in the framework of values that had developed in the nineteenth century. More than simply a reaction against modernity, this effort sought to develop new educational mechanisms to stem the erosion of moral training and preserve traditional values. Usually rallying around one of several programs of "character education," those who favored this approach attempted to retain a central place in the school for the teaching of specific virtues and the cultivation of the traits of good character. The other approach, the product of the progressive education movement, denigrated both the teaching of specific moral tenets and the cultivation of particular character traits and emphasized instead a more flexible and critical approach to moral education. Deeply skeptical of both traditional moral education and the new schemes of character education, progressives believed that modern society required a radically new approach to morality, and they sought to create a moral education that would meet the evolving needs of an ever-changing order. Finally, outside the public school, religious educators followed a third path, continuing to argue the necessity of grounding moral education in the tenets of faith and refusing to compromise with the accelerating trends toward secularization of education.

The divergence of views among public educators appeared as early as the first decade of the century, but progressive voices began to receive a significant hearing only in the mid-1920s. Until then, the effort to preserve traditional values through character education held at least an uneasy dominance in educational discourse and made a substantial impact on actual classroom practice. Religious schools remained strong and defiant throughout the first four decades of the century, offering an ongoing, though often quiet, critique of the efforts of both camps of moral educators in the schools.

The Effort to Preserve Character

The effort to promote character education programs was less a well-organized movement with a clear rationale than a diffuse attempt to preserve traditional values and ensure a place for moral training in the program of the public school. Although the campaign had the support of many prominent educators, especially in the first two decades of the century, its strongest leadership came from outside the established circle of major educational figures. From the beginning the movement had its greatest successes at the local level rather than in the great national forums of educational discourse, winning impressive support from state legislatures, state and city schools boards, private benefactors, and a variety of newspapers and popular magazines.

Always more programmatic than theoretical, the character education movement built not so much on a thorough and coherent analysis of social change as on a vague sense that modern society presented new challenges to important values and required a strong effort to preserve character. Supporters worried that as youngsters prepared for their narrow occupations in a highly differentiated and segmented society they would lose their moral bearings and perhaps even their physical and mental well-being. One danger of modern schooling was that it would develop a "one-sided efficiency," fitting students for their particular niches in a highly specialized society but neglecting "the body and the character" and stunting the ability of the individual "to stand alone as a thinking, upright citizen."[2]

Equally threatening to character were the new freedoms of the era. Vice may have been no worse than in the nineteenth century, but now it took place away from the scrutiny of home and community. Even worse, the traditional cultural and social sanctions against it had weakened as many modern Americans dismissed older proscriptions as mere prudery. With the spread of modernism in religion and the continuing secularization of society, fear of eternal punishment lost some of its power to divert men and women from pleasures that were increasingly available and alluring. The "day of science," declared one state teacher's manual, "has taken away from mankind most of the fears that once censored his conduct."[3]

Most champions of character education sought not to turn back the clock but rather to master the new era, to create a program of moral education that would prepare people to operate under the altered circumstances of the twentieth century without losing their integrity and without falling victim to the worst temptations of the day. Few of them viewed their effort as a rearguard action against modernity; instead, they believed that traditional values and modern economic and social organization were entirely compatible as long as children were properly prepared to live ethical lives in the new order.

Champions of character education developed a program only slowly. In the first decade of the century, those who worried about the place of moral education in modern schooling proposed a hodgepodge of remedies. Some favored specific courses in ethics or in "manners and morals" to supplement the usual work of the classroom. Milton Fairchild, for example, spent his early years in what became a lifetime of efforts in behalf of character education developing lantern slides designed to enhance the teaching of moral values. Others simply tried to shore up and extend the characteristic approaches of nineteenth-century moral education, paying increasing attention to the adolescent years and the rapidly growing junior and senior high schools.

By the middle of the second decade of the century, a more coherent program had emerged. Heavily influenced by a variety of reforms outside the school, especially the creation of such youth organizations as the Boy Scouts, 4–H clubs, and Campfire Girls, the new approach to character education emphasized the use of elaborate codes of conduct and the careful cultivation of group processes designed to encourage good behavior and moral growth. The hope of reformers was to turn traditional values into a modern creed and to use the vast new socializing powers of the school to create character as well as social and vocational competence.

It was the use of character codes that most clearly set these reformers off from the progressives. These codes were essentially lists of virtues, sometimes presented in the form of laws or pledges and designed to provide a focus for moral education both in and outside the classroom. The most influential, and one of the earliest, of the codes was written in response to a competition sponsored by the Character Education Association, a private organization created in 1911 and headed by Milton Fairchild. Authored by William Hutchins and published in 1917, the "Children's Morality Code" outlined "ten laws of right living": self-control, good health, kindness, sportsmanship, self-reliance, duty, reliability, truth, good workmanship, and teamwork. Directed at physical and mental hygiene as well as at moral development, the laws provided codes of behavior in each area. The law of reliability, for example, read:

The Good American Is Reliable

Our country grows great and good as her citizens are able more fully to trust each other. Therefore:

1. I will be honest, in word and in act. I will not lie, sneak, or pretend nor will I keep the truth from those who have a right to it.
2. I will not do wrong in the hope of not being found out. I cannot hide the truth from myself and cannot often hide it from others.
3. I will not take without permission what does not belong to me.
4. I will do promptly what I have promised to do. If I have made a foolish promise, I will at once confess my mistake, and I will try to make good any harm which my mistake may have caused. I will so speak and act that people will find it easier to trust each other.[4]

Many schools across the country quickly adopted the Hutchins code as a focus for their character training, sometimes using the code in its original form, sometimes modifying it in minor ways. Boston schools, for example, added a "law of obedience" to the code and made it the center of their program of moral instruction in the 1920s and early 1930s. Similar codes emerged from other sources—from city school superintendents, state school boards, even from *Colliers* magazine, which distributed a third of a million copies of its code to the nation's schools. All of these codes extolled the traditional virtues, and they differed only in the smallest details. Indeed, some school systems used the codes virtually interchangeably.

Educators expected moral codes to prompt teachers to attend to the development of character and to provide themes for instruction. In Boston, the School Committee published elaborate guides for teachers and encouraged schools to emphasize one law each month. In Birmingham, Alabama schools stressed one virtue each year, covering its particular code in the twelve years of schooling. The codes provided a focus for more than formal instruction. They formed the themes of posters in the classrooms and hallways, and they were emphasized in extracurricular activities. Thus, a school focusing on the virtue of loyalty might assign readings chosen to illustrate the theme and display banners with such slogans as "When a Man thinks, lives, and says 'WE,' he's Loyal." To help teach thrift, Birmingham schools encouraged children to open bank accounts, sell newspapers and surplus coat hangers, create book exchanges, and form budgeting clubs. The aim was to use the codes as a way of suffusing every facet of school life with moral education.[5]

If codes provided the substantive focus of moral education in this scheme, group activities offered the preferred method. Unlike nineteenth-century educators who usually viewed the classroom as a collection of individuals, each of whom learned values through direct contact with textbook and teacher, these twentieth-century reformers emphasized the importance of the group in the educational process. Impressed both by the importance of teamwork in modern forms of production and by new psychological theories about the formation of social instincts, these educators expected group interactions to play a vital role in developing character. Without ever giving up their own authority in the educational process, they sought to mobilize the power of peer influence to encourage moral development.

The reform in methods occurred both in and outside the classroom, with teachers now exploiting a whole variety of opportunities to place students in social situations that could be structured to produce moral development. Following the lead of the scouting movement, reformers were especially fond of student clubs. Sometimes the clubs were created within classes where students would adopt constitutions and creeds and pledge to cultivate such virtues as thrift, industry, honesty, and loyalty. For ex-

ample, an elementary school class in Norfolk, Virginia created an elaborate constitution for its Hustling Citizens' League whose object was to "have
a better system of working together, better laws, better organizations, and
better citizens; and to be a good example for the younger citizens of our
school, teaching them to be kind and just to one another."[6] Classes in many
other schools across the nation followed the suggestions of the National
Character Institution and created clubs called "Uncle Sam's Boys and
Girls," which not only promoted the usual virtues but even helped discipline their own members.

Outside the classroom, clubs played an even greater role. Not only did
schools open their facilities to local youth organizations but they created
an array of clubs of their own. Lincoln High School in Ferndale, Michigan,
for example, had large Hi-Y and Girl Reserves clubs, both of which combined recreational activities with work for local charitable causes.[7] In
Nebraska the state plan for character education called for schools to open
chapters of the Knighthood of Youth, a club that used medieval ritual to
attract students and prepare them for good citizenship. And in Boston some
schools even organized clubs around the cultivation of particular virtues:
the Courtesy Club, the Prompt Club, the Thrift Club, and the like. Especially in high schools, students across the country were encouraged to join
clubs that were expected to make a significant contribution to the development of character.[8]

In emphasizing group activities, character educators sought to use peer
influence without surrendering adult authority. Teachers were expected
to exercise a close supervision of all clubs and to orchestrate group activities to achieve the desired educational effect. Thus, the Nebraska character education plan called for the extensive use of projects to encourage moral
growth: "The teacher, with the assistance of the officers of Uncle Sam's
Club, will devise character projects to be carried out by the club which will
give expression to and tend to form habits in accordance with the important moral ideals. For example, appreciation of the right of the aged to
courtesy and respect will be developed by getting the club to appoint a
committee to perform acts of courtesy and service toward some aged person of the neighborhood." Similarly, should students show tendencies toward thievery or dishonesty, the teacher would mobilize the club to take
action: "The right and wrong of neighborhood stealing and suppression
of petty stealing by club members from nearby stores will be determined
and carried out through a court of justice organized by the club judge, under
advice from the teacher."[9]

One advantage of the use of clubs was that it allowed schools to offer
differentiated moral education to boys and girls. Although the two sexes
learned many common values, especially at the elementary school level,

educators in this era believed that boys and girls, especially in their adolescent years, required a distinctly different moral training. For girls, the traditional domestic virtues—sexual purity, gentleness, meekness, and the like—continued to be relevant, since Americans still expected most women to be mainly suited for life in the family. For boys, the needs of the modern era suggested a more complicated moral education, one that prepared them for a complex world of work as well as for life in the family.[10]

What made this a special challenge for educators was the widespread belief that the extension of schooling into adolescence posed a threat to the masculinity of boys. In an earlier era, boys had been able to balance the feminized moral education of the elementary school with an adolescence that took them rapidly into more masculine worlds of apprenticeship or work. Now an extended stay in schools threatened to weaken the development of masculine traits that made for success in the acquisitive, competitive world of work. With the family, the Sunday school, and the elementary school all dominated by women, educators sought to create in the high schools some outlet for boyish instincts and some mechanism to help shape a "muscular morality" that would equip young men to at once compete in the world of business and have the courage to fight the great social evils of the day.

Clubs offered one important opportunity for this kind of differentiated training, and many clubs were reserved exclusively for boys. The Hi-Y Club, for example, was the high school wing of the YMCA, which had long helped young men to negotiate the transition into adulthood. Interscholastic athletics offered an even better opportunity, and character educators went to extraordinary lengths to encourage the development of sports programs in high schools. They placed special faith in team sports such as football, where boys could find a useful outlet for their combative instincts and learn both the value of individual excellence and the importance of team effort, lessons thought to be essential for those who would live their lives in business, government, the professions, or the military.

Although extracurricular activities offered an especially important mechanism for character education, teachers had two other useful tools as well. First, in many schools, they could now include citizenship grades on their report cards. Although these grades were often little more than the deportment grades of the nineteenth century, some schools used them as measures of moral development. Second, where group instruction failed to achieve the desired effect, teachers could resort to the "case method" of moral education, which was in effect individual counseling for students judged to be delinquent.

The tendency of early twentieth-century reformers to use innovative pedagogical techniques to cultivate traditional virtues reflected their faith that modern life, for all of its novelty, could be managed in the framework of familiar values. The substance of their program was derived primarily from nineteenth-century morality. No one nourished on the McGuffey readers could have been surprised by the values these reformers sought to promote. Even their methods owed something to the nineteenth-century assumptions. Like their predecessors these reformers saw moral education as fundamentally a problem of motivation, not of ethical reasoning, and they sought to use every means available to them to ingrain good habits and to strengthen the will of students against the temptations of the day. To them, character was less a matter of making fine ethical distinctions than of having the resolve to do the right thing.

Yet despite their obvious debt to traditional moral education, these reformers were involved in something more than an effort to hold onto an outmoded past. They understood that the world had changed, and they were willing to make a range of accommodations to twentieth-century life. Few of them gave the morality codes religious sanction; most were willing to accept an entirely secular approach to moral education in the schools. Moreover, for all of their commitment to habit formation and absolute morality, they made at least a small place for the freedom of the learner, especially at the high school level, and leavened their instructional strategies with such open-ended techniques as debates and socialized recitations.

By promoting codes of conduct and urging the formation of clubs, early twentieth-century reformers offered an effective way to keep moral questions on the school's agenda and to bring some unity to curricula that seemed in constant danger of splintering. The program was concrete and comprehensible, and it won quick support from teachers and principals as well as educational leaders who operated at loftier levels. It provided students with a varied and thorough moral schooling in precisely the kinds of group settings that were characteristic of modern life, and it gave to the whole educational enterprise a pervasive moral tone. Its blending of physical and mental hygiene with moral and civic education—however peculiar by contemporary standards—provided a sense of wholeness to the idea of character and gave students a concrete way of understanding the connections between individual conduct and the public good.

At the same time, the failure of reformers to root their codes of conduct in an ethical system or to provide a way by which beliefs could be validated made their schemes unusually susceptible to the dictates of conventional morality. As critics pointed out, the codes and clubs so cherished by these reformers sometimes did little more than reinforce the standards of middle-class respectability. The scheme showed little tolerance for cultural diversity, and there can be no doubt that reformers expected it to play an important role in eliminating the differences that set immigrants off from the mainstream of American life. By combining moral prescriptions with a heavy-handed patriotism, reformers cast their lots with those who sought to deal with diversity by creating rigorous assimilationist schooling.

Nor did the reform encourage individual autonomy. Where individuals received special attention at all the purpose was always to return them to conformity with the general rules of behavior. Instructional strategies gave legitimacy to peer pressure and did little to develop the resources that would allow individuals to take bold stands against conventional standards. Moreover, because the scheme subordinated ethical reasoning to an emphasis on training of the will, it did little to encourage a broad, critical social vision and gave scant guidance to the individual faced with the problem of choosing from among conflicting values.

Its weakness notwithstanding, the effort to preserve traditional morality was pervasive in American schools in the first three decades of the century. By the mid-1920s, when the effort peaked, the use of codes was common in schools everywhere, and clubs designed in part to build character were virtually universal. However, this approach to moral education was never without its critics, and in the late 1920s its influence began a slow decline. The decline was partly a product of a growing impatience with conventional moral restraints, an impatience reflected in a variety of colorful ways in the 1920s. It was also partly the result of a concerted attack by progressive educators, who pressed their case with increasing urgency in the 1930s when economic and social dislocations seemed to call for a more critical approach to moral education. The publication in 1928–1930 of now-famous studies by Hugh Hartshorne and Mark A. May, which raised serious questions about the effectiveness of heavily didactic moral education programs, gave critics powerful ammunition and put champions of traditional morality in a defensive posture that they have struggled to escape ever since.[11]

The Progressive View

A radically different approach to moral education emerged from the efforts of a small but powerful group of reformers associated with the progressive education movement. First articulated at the turn of the century by such theorists as John Dewey, this approach gained supporters slowly until the mid-1920s when it was embraced by a growing number of liberal Protestant clergy, intellectual leaders, professional elites, and educators associated with major universities and large urban and suburban school systems. These progressives did not simply accept modernity; they believed that the new order offered hope of an unprecedented period of social and moral progress if only Americans would abandon the tyranny of tradition and strive for a just, productive, and democratic society through the application of science and reason to the complex problems of the day.

Progressive educators mounted a scathing attack on character education programs that emphasized the use of morality codes or the teaching of particular virtues. These programs, they argued, had produced poor results. "A knowledge of proverbs does not make good or efficient men," wrote one reformer. "Sancho Panza was running over with them. Nor does morality result from continual obedience to the dictates of conventionality."[12] New, "scientific" study, reformers believed, had raised serious questions about the ability of virtue-oriented character education either to affect the immediate behavior of children or to instill values that people would apply across the various dimensions of their lives. As Hugh Hartshorne, a progressive student of character education, put it: "If, for example, honesty is a unified character trait, and if all children either have it or do not have it, then we would expect to find children who are honest in one situation to be honest in all other situations and, *vice versa*, to find dishonest children to be deceptive in all situations. What we actually observe is that the honesty or dishonesty of a child in one situation is related to his honesty or dishonesty in another situation mainly to the degree that the situations have factors in common."[13]

The problem with conventional moral education was not simply its pedagogical ineffectiveness, however. Progressives argued that an emphasis on particular virtues provided a poor guide to ethical living in modern society. Simple aphorisms or codes of conduct were too crude, too rigid, to guide men and women in the highly specialized, ever-changing order of the modern world. "We need to see," declared Dewey, "that moral principles are not arbitrary, that they are not 'transcendental'; that the term 'moral' does not designate a special region or portion of life."[14] What was required was ethical flexibility and a sure sense of the relativity of values. Nowhere was the new standard proclaimed more forcefully than in the 1932 report of the Character Education Committee of the National Education Association's Department of Superintendence, which called for a moral education that taught students to apply values as particular situations dictated. "Relativity," the report declared, "must replace absolutism in the realm of morals as well as in the spheres of physics and biology. This of course does not involve the denial of the principle of continuity in human affairs. Nor does it mean that each generation must repudiate the system of values of its predecessors. It does mean, however, that no such system is permanent; that it will have to change and grow in response to experience."[15]

The necessity of relativity was in part the product of rapid change. Actions that produced ethical results in one era might not be so effective in another. "Character involves not only right intentions, but a certain degree of efficiency," wrote Dewey. "Now efficiency, as biologists have made us very well aware, is a problem of adaptation, of adjustment to the control of conditions. Are the conditions of modern life so clear and so settled that we know exactly what organs, what moral habits and methods, are necessary in order to get the maximum of efficiency?" Or as the 1932 Department of Superintendence report put it: "Analysis of adult activities today gives a list which may not constitute the best type of acts, even for today, and which is almost certain to be inadequate at some points for the changed social order."[16]

But the value of relativity was also related to the highly specialized and segmented character of modern life. What was moral in one sphere of life might be immoral in another, and men and women were expected to adjust their behavior as they moved from public to private realms, from the world of work to the world of the family, even from one business or profession to another. Ethical behavior was related to particular situations, and character education was meant to teach "constructive reactions" to life's extraordinarily varied contingencies. In the words of the Department of Superintendence, "The need for character is all bound up in the event itself. It is tangible and concrete and real. It cannot be escaped or relegated to copy books. Life is one situation after another, and each situation has possibilities of richer or poorer living, of greater or less integration of values."[17]

Rejecting the notion that the school should teach specific moral precepts or encourage particular traits, progressive educators hoped to cultivate in students both a quality of open-mindedness and a general ability to make moral judgments. Their model for ethical behavior was the disinterested expert, the professional who brought both a spirit of inquiry and a high level of competence to the solutions of problems. What worked in the world of science and technology, they believed, would work as well in the solution of other human problems, if only students could be taught moral imagination, "the ability to picture vividly the good or evil consequences to self and to others of any type of behavior."[18]

Although progressives viewed their approach to moral education as a comprehensive scheme, they consistently gave more attention to great social and political issues than to matters of private conduct. Reversing the emphasis of earlier moral educators, they expressed little interest in the drinking habits or sexual conduct of individuals as long as such personal behavior did not impede the ability to operate as intelligent and productive citizens. Character in this view was not a matter of adhering to some set of rules of upright conduct—that was mere Victorianism. Instead, character had to do with the ability to contribute to the creation of a more humane and democratic society. "The moral," wrote Dewey in an attack on virtue-centered character education, "has been conceived in too goody-goody a way. Ultimate moral motives and forces are nothing more or less than social intelligence—the power of observing and comprehending social situations,—and social power—trained capacities of control—at work in the service of social interest and aims."[19] Tired of what seemed to be the unnecessary restraints placed on personal behavior by nineteenth- and early twentieth-century moralists, progressives sought to give character education a decidedly more civic cast.

In viewing character as the ability to act efficiently and thoughtfully in the cause of social improvement, progressives gave new significance to the role of intellectual endeavor in moral education. The good citizen, in their scheme, was not simply the person with the right intentions and a strong will but someone who could understand the social world and carefully calculate the social consequences of actions. Yet what progressives sought was not intellectual endeavor of the traditional sort. Skeptical about the wisdom of the past, they turned not to established texts but rather to the methods of scientific inquiry and democratic decision-making, hoping to equip students with the intellectual skills that would allow them to deal constructively and creatively with the social problems of the day.

In keeping with these goals, progressives constructed a pedagogy that emphasized problem-solving and social learning. Instead of making inherited tradition the starting point of learning, they sought to build on the immediate experiences of the children. Using familiar problems from everyday life, they hoped to cultivate a mode of problem-solving that employed scientific reasoning and democratic deliberation. Thus, they sought to simulate in the classroom the kinds of challenges that students might encounter in the world of work or politics. They were especially fond of excursions that would allow children to observe adults at work and of projects that would require groups of students to work together on the solution of problems that resembled real-life situations.

Like so many other early twentieth-century educators, progressives believed that children learned best in groups, and they eagerly embraced such innovations as socialized discussion, dramatization, student clubs, and extracurricular activities. Their goals, however, differed from those of other reformers, and they gave group activities an entirely distinctive meaning. Unlike character educators who attempted to use group pressure to reinforce adult codes, progressives expected social learning to teach democratic decision-making and to help children break from tradition and create novel solutions of their own. In the traditional classroom, wrote Hartshorne, students were encouraged "to talk about codes already formulated, to criticize their own behavior in light of conventional standards, to debate whether imaginary characters presented in cases did right or wrong." In the progressive classroom, on the other hand, "life situations taken from the experience of the children of the group . . . are discussed not in terms of some preformulated code but in terms of the problems confronted, or the efforts made to solve these problems, of the success or failure met with, and of the principle of conduct suggested by the total experiences. From genuine intellectual effort of this sort in which the judgment of the pupils is respected, there may emerge a *working* ideal, in contrast with the set of idle, though pious, effusions of adults to which children have almost universally been invited to give lip service."[20]

Because they identified character as way of thinking rather than as a knowledge of particular virtues, progressives believed that all school subjects held the promise of providing moral education. In this respect, they joined other American educators in favoring a schooling that used a wide range of opportunities to shape character. At the same time, progressives had a special faith in the ability of the social studies to provide moral education, and they elevated social studies courses above the literary disciplines that had furnished much of the wisdom of earlier programs of character education. The social studies, they believed, would help promote social understanding, develop critical thinking, and make children sensitive to their social obligations. Especially promising, in their view, was the expanding-horizons approach to the social studies, an approach that began by exploring the familiar institutions of the local community and led by steps to the study of state, national, and international affairs. A near-perfect embodiment of progressive pedagogy, the expanding-horizons approach broke with the formal traditions of political economy and encouraged students to use their own experiences rather than classical theories as the building blocks for their moral and civic education.

As their radical pedagogy suggests, educational progressives sought a dramatic departure from traditional character education programs. Impressed by the novelty of modern industrial society and by a pace of change that seemed only to accelerate, they were committed to a profoundly new approach to morality and moral education. In many important respects, their scheme was an extraordinarily imaginative response to modernity. By emphasizing critical thinking, for example, progressives gave students a basis for questioning arbitrary authority, for abandoning outmoded traditions, and for meeting the novel challenges of a world in flux. By emphasizing ethical flexibility and sensitivity to situation, they prepared them to deal with the varying demands of a highly segmented society in which different arenas called for different moral responses. By teaching them to judge actions by social consequence, they gave them a new, purely secular standard by which to make moral decisions.

Yet, if progressive moral education avoided many of the pitfalls of traditional programs, it created some new ones of its own. By denigrating tradition, weakening the authority of adults, and giving new legitimacy to peer influence, progressivism left students vulnerable to the tyranny of both the immediate group and the present moment. It gave no more protection to the individual than did other twentieth-century approaches. Indeed, its child-centeredness left dissenting students without even the option of invoking adult authority against the power of their peers. "If one looks at it from the standpoint of the individual child," one critic of progressivism, Hannah Arendt, has written, "his chances to rebel or to do anything on his own hook are practically nil; . . . rather he is in the position, hopeless by definition, of a minority of one confronted by the absolute majority of all the others."[21]

Nor did progressivism insulate the school from the influence of conventional morality. As Michael Walzer has pointed out, children were even more likely than teachers to be carriers of conventionality. Thus, by weakening the authority of adults in the classroom, progressives made the school more sensitive than ever to the "transient concerns and values of the society."[22] Moreover, by making the immediate experience of the child the starting point of learning, progressives devalued both text and tradition, leaving students with a dearth of cultural materials from which to shape moral decisions. Although progressivism offered students a certain liberation from ancient dogmas, it provided them with far fewer resources for resisting the popular wisdom of their own time and place.

The vagueness of progressive prescriptions was another problem. Teachers found it difficult to provide a moral education that had no place for particular virtues: to teach a process of thinking without a specific content was a challenge many could simply not meet. In the absence of concrete guidance on the subject, it was easy to confuse trivial classroom discussions with meaningful moral deliberation. The problem was only confounded by the failure of progressives to offer a clear theory of moral development or to pay adequate attention to purely private conduct and its relationship to the social good.

Because progressive moral education had few easily identifiable programmatic markers, its influence is not easy to measure. State and local school board reports as well as scholarly literature showed a widespread acquaintance with the major tenets of the theory as early as the 1920s and a growing support for it during the 1930s. Many progressive high schools and some city systems made deliberate efforts to encourage the new approach. Denver schools, for example, gradually abandoned their virtue-centered approaches and made the social studies curriculum the core of their efforts to shape character. More often, however, schools offered a hodgepodge of moral education programs, with theoretically incompatible approaches sometimes existing side by side. Rarely did progressive moral education root out and replace virtue-centered programs; rather, it functioned as a continuing alternative, one of two widely accepted responses to the problem of moral education in the modern world of the early twentieth century.

The Claims of Religion

In marked contrast to nineteenth-century educators, the men and women who shaped the dominant approaches to moral education in the early twentieth century justified their schemes on purely secular grounds. Although many had strong religious views of their own, they largely abandoned the notion that schools should teach a nondenominational Christianity. They were, to be sure, far from rigorous in their secularism, often looking the other way when some schools continued to sanction prayer and Bible-reading, but their bias was toward church-state separation and they rarely made common cause with evangelical or fundamentalist groups who sought to reverse the drift of public policy on the matter. Mainline Protestants, who had favored nondenominational religion in nineteenth-century schools, now accepted a more secular approach, and they drew growing support from Jews and nonbelievers. More than ever to them, religion was a matter for Sunday school, church, and home.

As indicated in chapter 3, however, many Catholics and Lutherans, as well as some Jews and evangelical Protestants, resisted these efforts to separate religion and moral education. From varying perspectives, they offered a sharp critique of the secularism embodied in both progressive education and virtue-centered moral education approaches. The strongest and best-organized dissent came from Catholics, who continued the argument made in the nineteenth century that moral education required a grounding in the tenets of faith. Catholics took particularly strong exception to progressive theories. They objected to the rigorous secularism of progressivism: to its slavish commitment to science, its failure to deal with the matter of will, and its neglect of personal morality. They associated its influence with permissiveness in child rearing and schooling and held it partially responsible for youthful rebellion and delinquency and for the declining sexual mores of the society.

Catholics were considerably more sympathetic to the character education movement, but even that approach, with all its support for traditional values, did not escape their criticism. In reviewing the Nebraska character education program, the Reverend Luke L. Mandeville, diocesan superintendent of schools in Lincoln, took sharp exception to the claim that a "commission of high-minded men and women . . . could supply us with a code of morals better perhaps than any code yet devised." "This of course," wrote Mandeville, "seems to do scant justice to two considerations imperative in Catholic school teaching: first, that Moses did not devise the decalogue but received it from the Lord on Mount Sinai; secondly, that far from taking counsel from the moral opinions of the majority, the Great Lawgiver had to write, 'With most of them God was not well pleased.' "[23]

At odds with the public school on the matter of religion and disturbed by the growing secularism in character education programs, Catholics, Lutherans, and scattered other sects continued to support parochial schools—often at extraordinary expense. Only on the matter of high schools did they make some accommodations. Where the cost of separate secondary schools was unbearable, many parishes allowed youngsters to attend public high schools instead, assured that children had at least received a strong early religious training. In places where Catholic children attended public schools in large numbers, their parents and priests often became active in school politics, usually in support of released time for religious education—a practice that was common in Boston and many other heavily Catholic areas in the 1930s and 1940s.

The growing secularism of the public school elicited a different response from some evangelical and fundamentalist Protestants. Far less organized than Catholics or Missouri Synod Lutherans and lacking a tradition of parochial schooling, they focused their efforts on retaining a place for religion in public education and on keeping out anything that might either challenge their faith or degrade the morals of their children. They resisted any effort to limit prayer and Bible-reading in the schools, opposed the teaching of evolution, and exercised a careful scrutiny over the moral content of schoolbooks.

Evangelicals and fundamentalists won countless victories on the local level. Where they were strong—especially in parts of the rural South—they were able to exercise a measure of censorship of schoolbooks, to drive out teachers who failed to live up to their demanding ideological and moral standards, and to keep a secure place for prayer, Bible-reading, and religious ceremonies. However, they rarely played a significant role in the various national organizations that established the broad outlines of public educational policy in these years. Often operating at the margins of society, they were, in the end, able to do little to stem the unmistakable movement in the early twentieth century toward a purely secular moral education in the public school.

Moral Education and the Transformation of Higher Education

The forces that transformed elementary and secondary education in the late nineteenth and early twentieth centuries had an equally dramatic effect on colleges and universities. Change was apparent as early as the 1870s, when the expansion of knowledge and a growing demand for professional training began to shatter the tightly prescribed curriculum that had characterized higher education in the antebellum era. The ancient dream of broadly educated people who could integrate the spheres of learning and develop a comprehensive view of the world quickly disappeared as a new generation of educators began to emphasize the production of new knowledge and the preparation of students for specific careers. As research and specialization came to be the dominating ideals of great universities, educators found it increasingly difficult to integrate intellectual and moral concerns, and character education moved to the margins of higher education in all but the smallest and most religious of the colleges.

A vast expansion of the curriculum was the most visible sign of change. As knowledge grew and inquiry became more specialized, most traditional studies gave way to a variety of new, more focused disciplines. Moral philosophy was one of the first victims of this process, as its formerly broad domain came to be occupied by such disciplines as ethics, psychology, sociology, and political science. For more than a hundred years, moral philosophy had put the finishing touch on the education of all college students and had set the tone for the whole curriculum; in the late nineteenth century, it largely disappeared, leaving students without a capstone course and colleges without a formal way to complete the process of moral education.

The very structure of the modern university made it difficult to find an adequate substitute for the moral education provided by the antebellum college. A growing emphasis on research encouraged ambitious members of the faculty to limit their time with undergraduate students and to focus their intellectual activities on narrow realms where they could produce new knowledge and establish reputations as experts. As disciplines splintered and fields within disciplines grew more narrow, professors were increasingly unwilling to deal with broad moral questions. By the rules of the new academic game, their task was to attend to the issues that members of the discipline defined as important, and they risked their scholarly reputations if they ventured beyond these boundaries to engage in serious moral and political debate.

The structural impediments to moral education were reinforced in the twentieth century by changing intellectual fashions, especially the growing importance of positivism, a view that devalued theology and metaphysics and regarded the findings of empirical science as the only knowledge worth having. Positivism had a particular impact on the social sciences, where it sharpened the bias against dealing with questions of ethics or values in the classroom. Behaviorism in psychology and the growing use of quantification in other disciplines made it difficult to talk about such matters as choice, purpose, or consciousness, staple topics in older schemes of moral education. Instead, tough-minded social scientists dealt with a world of measurable facts and won their reputations not for their ability to probe ethical issues but rather for their mastery of the intricate methodologies of modern research.[24]

In opting to emphasize scientific knowledge and to place value questions off limits, positivists were not necessarily expressing a moral callousness. Rather, they were acting on the assumption that the problems of the modern world were more technical than moral in nature. What was needed was not contemplation or exhortation but scientific study and the application of expertise. "The whole drift of present educational thinking," observed one scholar, "is to produce the efficient man—the man related by forceful deeds to the world without."[25] It was this faith in the progressive influence of the efficient man that allowed positivists to embrace a "value-free" learning without ever losing their sense of moral purpose.

Despite the idealism that underlay it, positivism worked against every effort to preserve a place for moral education. It had equally corrosive effects on religion. Although many scholars and students alike retained a private religious faith, post-Darwinian science and social science left little room for the serious discussion of the supernatural. Students who had once found support for their faith in every corner of the curriculum increasingly had to seek special instruction in departments of religion or in courses on the "Evidences of Christianity." Even these options became limited in the twentieth century as a growing number of colleges severed their denominational ties and many state universities abolished courses in religion out of deference to the doctrine of church-state separation. Although chapel services continued on most campuses, formal support for religion declined dramatically except in institutions that retained their ecclesiastical affiliations.

Preserving a Place for Moral Education

The forces that threatened religion and moral education on campuses were powerful throughout the late nineteenth and early twentieth centuries, but they did not go unchallenged. A substantial number of Americans, both in and outside higher education, refused to accept the implications of positivism and worked hard to reserve a place for moral and spiritual matters in colleges and universities. Indeed, as Julie A. Reuben has pointed out, each wave of university reform was invested with the hope that an effective modern moral education would result.[26] Most educators understood and accepted the decline of moral philosophy, but they attempted to find other studies that might provide comparable instruction for modern students. Two clusters of reformers devised the most widely supported approaches to moral education in the modern college and university: progressives, who sought to draw on science and social science to fashion a new, explicitly modern moral sensibility, and champions of liberal culture and general education, who found in the humanities the best hope for cultivating virtuous men and women.

Although progressives hoped that a broad spectrum of courses in science and social science would promote their particular notions about modernity and morality, they paid special attention to courses in ethics, hoping to use them as the cornerstone of their effort to build a moral education that would prepare students for the shifting ethical demands of contemporary society. Progressives walked a middle line in higher education, rejecting the notion of unchanging ideals but also resisting the kind of positivism that denied a place for the study of normative questions. Not surprisingly, John Dewey was in the forefront of the progressive campaign. He not only coauthored (with James H. Tufts) one of the most widely used textbooks in ethics but also campaigned tirelessly for an approach that emphasized the situational character of ethical problems and the need to give students the moral sensitivity and intellectual capacity to deal with the ever-changing challenges of the modern world.[27]

Dewey and his progressive colleagues sought not only to revitalize the undergraduate course in ethics but also to promote the creation of special courses in professional ethics. Convinced that ethical challenges varied across occupations, they argued that students needed to study the particular moral dilemmas they were likely to encounter in such fields as law, business, and medicine. By combining work in general ethical theory with the study of the special cases confronting particular professions, progressives hoped to produce men and women who could bring both expertise and moral sensitivity to the solution of modern social problems.

Progressives had their strongest influence at the turn of the century when scientists and social scientists were still engaged in consideration of moral questions. Yet even then, their reform achieved only a partial success. Their particular ethical theories, to be sure, received a prompt and sympathetic hearing and even came to dominate the ethics textbooks of the 1920s and 1930s, but the stature of ethics courses themselves remained low. The undergraduate course continued to be an elective in most institutions, and only a small minority of students chose to enroll in it. Although a growing number of professional schools followed the prompting of progressives and created special courses in ethics and professional responsibility, they frequently staffed them poorly and rarely gave them an important place in their curricula.

By the late 1930s progressives faced an even more daunting problem as the field of ethics itself began to come under the influence of philosophical analysts, who brought to ethics some of the skepticism about the discussion of moral issues that had become ingrained in the social sciences. Philosophical analysts subordinated normative questions to metaethical issues, focusing less on questions of right or wrong than on the language and meaning of ethical discourse. As the influence of the analysts grew, students found even courses in ethics a hostile environment for the study of the practical moral dilemmas that confronted them. "The result," as Bernard Rosen has written, "was an academic life in which there were few forums for the discussion of normative issues, and almost no legitimate place for the discussion of normative ethical theories."[28]

As progressives struggled to use science and social science to revitalize moral education, others placed their hopes for moral education in a revival of the humanities. Like the proponents of virtue-centered moral education in elementary and secondary schools, they believed that history, literature, and other liberal studies contained ancient truths that retained their relevance in a modern world. The earliest articulation of this view in the modern era came in the late nineteenth century and had about it both an elitist and antiprogressive cast. Reacting sharply against specialization and careerism, the early champions of liberal culture sought to produce men and women with a breadth of vision, an altruistic spirit, a disdain for materialism, and an aristocratic appreciation for leisure and high culture.[29]

Although liberal culturalists were for a while able to reserve a place in the curriculum for the discussion of virtue, they lost ground steadily after the first decade of the century as their aristocratic pretensions appeared increasingly quaint and dysfunctional. In their place, however, emerged another group of theorists who brought a more democratic spirit to the task of defending the humanities. Associated with what came to be called the "general education movement" in the 1920s and 1930s, these theorists argued that all students should be required to take a core of courses that acquainted them with the main streams of Western culture and prepared them for lives of useful citizenship. What was needed, in this view, was not a small class of leaders schooled in the manners and morality of the gentlemanly class but rather a broad range of people who understood Western values and who could apply their knowledge to the moral questions of the modern world.

The effect of the general education movement was to shore up the place of the humanities and to reverse some of the worst effects of an elective system that had allowed many students to virtually circumvent liberal studies. In response to the movement, some universities began to require courses in Western civilization; others developed more rigorous distribution requirements that compelled students to include at least some courses in the humanities in their programs of study. Yet, as Douglas Sloan has pointed out, general education was "something of a rearguard action," and it never succeeded in creating a completely safe curricular home for moral education.[30] Its local successes—in places like Columbia, Chicago, and St. John's College of Annapolis—were impressive, but students in many institutions of higher education could still pursue their special studies without learning much about Western values or engaging in the serious study of moral issues.

Reformers also found it difficult to ensure that courses in the humanities would address moral questions in any systematic way. Instructors enjoyed a wide latitude in the choice of topics and texts, and not all of them were interested in the moral dimensions of their subjects. Professors in the humanities were under no less pressure to publish than their counterparts in the sciences and social sciences, and their disciplines did not always support inquiry into moral issues. Nor were reformers able to create clusters of required courses that together might offer a well-integrated moral education, except in a few special schools. Thus, while classes in the humanities remained more open to moral discourse than most other classes, they fell far short of providing the kind of thorough moral education that reformers had hoped for.

Character and Campus Life

Unable to achieve a satisfactory character education in the classroom, university administrators increasingly focused their efforts on the extracurriculum. As early as first decade of the twentieth century, they began to reassume control of extracurricular activities that had largely fallen into student hands in the late nineteenth century. Their aim was to turn student life into a means for moral instruction, and they began to exercise a much closer supervision of a range of student activities, from intercollegiate athletics to fraternity parties. They undertook a vast new construction of dormitories, where students could be more closely watched and instructed, and they encouraged the creation of residential colleges and social clubs in hopes of creating a sense of community and moral purpose. Many also supported the activities of the YMCA and the newly emerging campus pastorates such as the Newman Club or the Wesley Foundation.

Despite their best efforts, however, administrators failed to capture campus life for the cause of moral education. Many students bridled at the new scrutiny of college officials and continued to use student activities as a way to break away from traditional restraints and explore new freedoms. As Paula Fass and others have pointed out, student frivolity did not necessarily reflect a rejection of adult values, but it did indicate that a substantial number of students no longer accepted the college campus as a proper place for the airing of their religious or moral views.[31] Like the positivists on the faculty, they chose instead to treat value questions as purely private matters and keep them off the agenda of American college life.

Conclusion: The Legacies of Modernization

On the eve of the Second World War, Americans could look back at a wrenching half-century of modernization. For all of its promise of material abundance and expanded freedom, the process had left many troubling questions about morality and moral education. Despite sweeping efforts to reform moral education, especially in the public schools, Americans continued to worry about the character of their young. Moreover, they remained torn about the proper approach to moral education in the new environment of the twentieth century. Although progressive approaches had won increasing favor in the public schools of the 1930s, older programs of character education continued to have their strong champions. Sometimes the contending parties were able to reach accommodations within particular schools, but they were never able to resolve their fundamental differences and the debates between them continued to be fierce.

Nor did the process of modernization resolve differences about the connections between religion and moral education. Although a growing number of Catholic and Lutheran parents sent their children to public schools, church leaders in both sects continued to prefer private institutions where religious and moral instruction could be combined. Critical of any purely secular approach to moral education, they continued a long tradition of criticism of the public school. Ironically, they were joined in these years by some evangelical Protestants, who were newly alarmed by the secularization of public education. Once uncritical supporters of the public school, these evangelicals now scrutinized it carefully and undertook a vigorous, though decentralized, campaign to resist every effort to restrict nondenominational religious activities in the classroom.

Leaders in higher education were as divided as their counterparts in elementary and secondary schools. Here modernization had a dramatic effect, leading some to believe that colleges and universities could focus their efforts entirely on research and professional preparation while leaving moral education to other institutions in the society. The enormous prestige of expertise and the growing influence of a "value-free" science and social science made it tempting to abandon altogether traditional responsibilities for character development. Yet a large number of educators were unwilling to take that step. Instead, they searched for new approaches to the problem of moral education in modern society and developed responses that bore some resemblance to the options devised for elementary and secondary schools. Progressives proposed to use ethics courses as a way of teaching a moral sensitivity to the changing contingencies of modern life, while proponents of liberal culture and general education sought a more virtue-centered approach. While these two responses influenced a broad range of public and private institutions, many church-affiliated colleges and universities carried on a third tradition which continued to combine religion and moral education in a way that was not fundamentally different from the practices of parochial schools.

CHAPTER FIVE

Decline and Revival, 1945–Present

For those who labored to preserve a place for moral education in colleges and universities, the 1940s and 1950s were a time of continuing disappointment, but champions of moral education in elementary and secondary schools entered the postwar era with a sense of fulfillment and hope. Both the Second World War and the early stages of the Cold War seemed to emphasize the importance of character, at least in the education of children and adolescents, and schools offered a rich variety of activities designed to promote moral and civic growth. Campaigns to collect scrap metal, purchase saving stamps, and sell government bonds helped schools combine the shaping of individual character with the teaching of civic responsibility and gave students a sense of connection between their personal efforts and the national destiny. Both progressives and advocates of more traditional character-building schemes found much to support in these programs, and the sharp debates of the 1920s and 1930s softened in the 1940s and 1950s. Leading educational associations now articulated a conventional wisdom that made a place for both the transmission of specific values and the teaching of ethical flexibility, offering just enough to each side of the earlier debates to promote a comfortable sense of accommodation, if not quite consensus, on the place of moral education in the American school.

Just as moral education seemed to have achieved a secure place in modern American schooling, however, new forces began to erode it. In the 1940s and 1950s, the challenges were subtle and indirect, hardly noticeable to many educators; but by the 1960s deliberate moral education was in full-scale retreat in the nation's schools. Throughout the 1960s and 1970s a variety of forces challenged the place of moral education, and schools either rapidly adopted a careful neutrality on moral questions or became entirely indifferent to them. The decline was dramatic, and most educators and policymakers acceded to it with only a subdued note of regret. A few Americans, however, were alarmed by this development and began in the mid-1960s a quest for a restoration of moral education in the schools. Although that quest has so far produced more rhetoric than action, it has reversed the decline of moral education, evoked discussion of a variety of new approaches, and created at least the possibility that questions of character and morality might once again enjoy a primary place on the agenda of American education.

Reaffirmations and Accommodations

Most educators found in the events of the 1940s and 1950s a powerful rationale for reaffirming the importance of moral education in the schools. They viewed both the Second World War and the Cold War as moral contests in which the values of democracy and decency were arrayed against the forces of authoritarianism and evil, and they expected the classroom to play an important role in the battle. As Americans united against the international perils, they subordinated the sharp differences about moral education that had split them in the interwar years. An eclectic and accommodating spirit characterized both formal statements about moral education and actual school practice, as educators drew some of their schemes from virtue-centered approaches and others from progressivism. Especially during the Second World War, the involvement of students in character-building community activities gave comfort to moral educators of all persuasions and muddied the differences between them.

The texture of the new spirit was perhaps conveyed most clearly in the 1951 report of the Educational Policies Commission of the National Education Association and the American Association of School Administrators entitled *Moral and Spiritual Values in the Public Schools*. Fashioned by a group of prominent American educators, this report reaffirmed the importance of moral education in the postwar era and tried to define a balanced program that would simultaneously teach certain values considered central to the American experience and promote the flexibility and open-mindedness necessary to adapt in a fast-changing world.

Drawing on a newly accentuated sense of American uniqueness, the Educational Policies Commission argued that educators could identify "a generally accepted body of values" that should be transmitted in the nation's schools. Among these "essential" values were respect for the individual personality, devotion to truth, commitment to brotherhood, and acceptance of individual moral responsibility. Schools, they argued, had both the right and the responsibility to inculcate these values in their students. Moreover, in a departure from interwar secularism, the commission urged schools to promote spiritual as well as moral values—to encourage education about religion, to permit children to express their religious opinions "in a natural way," and to allow teachers to show their approval of student participation in religious activities.[1]

Despite its willingness to endorse the teaching of specific values, the Educational Policies Commission stopped short of giving those values universal or transcendent meaning. Like the progressives of an earlier day, the commission treated values as the product of particular historical circumstances and proclaimed the need for periodic reformulations. In fact, the commission recommended that parents and teachers confer to establish the agenda for moral education: "It is especially important that the needs and problems of each community, as well as the probable public reaction, be taken into account from the outset. The very process of participation in preparing, considering, and approving such a list should help teachers and parents reflect on moral and spiritual values in ways which, to some of them at least, will be novel and stimulating."[2]

Most established educational leaders warmly endorsed the moderate formulations of the Educational Policies Commission, but several vocal theorists outside the mainstream of American education tried to revive enthusiasm for an older form of character education, one that emphasized the development of specific character traits and the use of formal codes of conduct. Financed largely by private philanthropic foundations, these theorists were unwilling to make significant compromises with progressive notions. Instead they worked out of a strong religious commitment, and they continued to regard values as transcendent. In their view, nothing less than direct instruction in the eternal verities could offer an adequate moral education.

Among the most important of these conservative theorists were Henry Lester Smith, dean of the Indiana University School of Education, and Ernest Ligon, director of the Character Education Project at Union College. Smith, whose work was sponsored by the Palmer Foundation of Texarkana, Arkansas, favored a schooling, especially at the elementary level, that used a variety of techniques to teach morality and patriotism. He proposed the continued use of morality codes, argued for "lessons developed around selected character traits," and found no problem with the use of religious exercises where communities did not object.[3]

Ligon was a more complex figure. A graduate of Yale Divinity School, he studied with Jean Piaget in the 1930s and became a student of the psychology of moral education. A deeply religious man, Ligon also had a powerful faith in the ability of social science to strengthen techniques of moral education. Calling scientific method "one form of prayer," Ligon believed that his research would enable religious educators and character-building agencies to "double their effectiveness every decade for the foreseeable future."[4] Supported generously by the Lilly Endowment and encouraged by Eli Lilly himself, Ligon did not share progressive notions about the evolution of values.[5] Instead, he sought to use science to find better ways to teach eternal truths and develop proper character traits.

Although he was familiar with social-scientific critiques of trait-based moral education, Ligon continued to believe that modern science would support the teaching of particular virtues.

Despite his academic position, his large staff, and his access to enormous financial resources, Ligon exercised only a small influence. His views were best known in religious education circles, and his methods were most often used in church school classes. Although a few schools experimented with his approach, his work had little general impact on public education. His idiosyncratic approach to religion and science discredited him among both mainstream Protestant theorists and established social-scientific circles. A quaint, fringe figure, Ligon worked hard to keep alive an older tradition of moral education, but in the end did little to disturb the more moderate accommodations recommended by the Educational Policies Commission.

Moral Education in Decline: The Early Stages

Despite the lofty declarations of the Educational Policies Commission and the dedicated work of such outsiders as Smith and Ligon, the place of moral education in the school began to erode in the 1940s and 1950s. The subtle decline was not the result of a concerted attack on moral education but rather the product a gradual shift in educational priorities. Without ever fully confronting the implications for moral education, postwar Americans began to demand that schools emphasize high-level academic and cognitive skills, often at the expense of the various forms of moral, civic, and social education that had been emphasized by earlier generations. A variety of well-placed Americans called for a new emphasis on intellectual development through study of the hard disciplines, and a noisy attack on progressivism belittled traditional concern with the "whole child." Educators who had once prided themselves on their ability to reshape character now paid more attention to the SAT scores of their students, and middle-class parents scrambled to find schools that would give their children the best chance to qualify for elite colleges and universities, even if that effort required moving the household to an expensive suburb.

The growing emphasis on the cognitive dimensions of education and the subtle neglect of the moral, particularly in public education, is not easily explained; but three developments seem to have played a significant role. First, a growing need for high-level technical and scientific skills—associated especially with revolutions in electronics, physics, and medicine—led Americans to call upon schools for a greater emphasis on intellectual achievement and basic academic skills. Now individual success appeared to have more to do with skill than with character or personality, and ambitious parents began to insist that schools respond to the new situation. As more and more professions raised educational requirements for entry and growing numbers of students aspired to college educations, schools responded by trimming "soft" courses and activities, where character education had often been offered, and by moving resources to college preparatory programs. Even in civics and social studies courses, which had once been havens for character education, reformers now subtly deemphasized prescriptive citizenship training in the interest of instruction that would give students the skills of the detached, professional social scientist.

A second force encouraging the shift in priorities was the emergence of a pervasive anticommunism that threatened to subsume other moral energies of the society and direct attention away from the issues that had been the focus of character education before 1945. Anticommunism proved to be a remarkably inclusive and unifying crusade, bringing together in a common cause a variety of interests who feared for the future of capitalism, democracy, or religion. Schools responded by reshaping moral and civic instruction to focus on the dangers of communism or, in some cases, by creating entirely new courses to prepare students to fight the totalitarian menace. These courses drew a sharp contrast between communist countries and the free world and promoted a relatively uncritical view of the United States as a land of individual rights and opportunity. The "Unit on Communism, Enemy of Democracy" required in Boston schools, for example, warned students to be wary of criticism of the United States from without and suspicious of divisive movements from within. In this atmosphere, teaching national loyalty and giving students the cognitive skills to contribute to the economic and military competition with the Soviets seemed to some educators to exhaust the school's responsibilities for character and citizenship education. Attention to more personal moral duties and more local civic responsibilities declined accordingly.

Finally, a growing tendency of Americans to draw sharp distinctions between private and public realms and to establish different behavioral norms for each sphere led many schools to avoid moral questions that might be considered primarily personal. Sharply accentuating a trend that had begun earlier, Americans of the postwar era increasingly thought of religion and morals as personal and private and assigned responsibility for them to home and church rather than to the school. New psychological theories that stressed the importance of shaping character in the first six years of life reinforced the trend, emphasizing the critical influence of the family and relieving the school of some of its former responsibilities. Parents of the day became increasingly confident in their ability to impart values and increasingly jealous of their prerogatives in the realm of personal morality, making them somewhat more likely than their predecessors to scrutinize and criticize the moral education provided by the schools.

The Eclipse of Moral Education

Priorities shifted slowly and unevenly in the 1940s and 1950s, and the place of moral education eroded only gradually. Those who neglected matters of character in those decades acted less out of disdain for moral education than out of the need to find more time for purely cognitive development. All of this changed in the 1960s and 1970s, however, when the retreat from moral education became both rapid and purposeful. To the older impulses that had worked to limit moral education were added a variety of new forces produced by one of the most tumultuous eras in American history. Educators who had once simply neglected moral education now began to regard it as problematic in and of itself—difficult to provide at best and a source of enormous controversy at worst. Faced with other knotty problems as well, most notably racial division, teachers and administrators were only too happy to flee from the task of moral education and return responsibility for character development to family and church.

The forces that made moral education so problematic for the public schools were the products of a number of social and cultural upheavals. The effort to end racial discrimination, the waging of an unpopular war, a deepening cultural pluralism, and a growing willingness to expand the range of acceptable personal conduct all worked to weaken the commitment of schools to moral education. The struggle to achieve racial equality and disputes over the Vietnam War were particularly divisive, giving a debilitating brittleness to social relations of the era. With deep suspicions now sharpening racial, ethnic, and class divisions, Americans lost faith in their ability to find common ground. Increasingly they sought to preserve a fragile peace by accepting differences and encouraging tolerance. In the process they elevated cultural relativism to a primary social value. Now Americans were to have wide latitude in their choice of lifestyles and in their choice of values, and any institution that tried to limit the options or arbitrate the differences risked aggravating the divisions of a tense, perhaps even potentially explosive, society.

Educators were among the first to feel the effects of the new social tensions and to express the popular relativism. Beginning with the civil rights movement, schools became a focus for the efforts to achieve new rights and protect old entitlements, and advocacy groups began to look over the shoulders of teachers and administrators with an intensity unprecedented in the twentieth century. The growing involvement of the federal government in education only complicated the problem, introducing an alien and often disruptive force into the traditionally local politics of public schooling. Increasingly on the defensive as they tried to balance the demands of competing constituencies, educators began to avoid controversy at almost any cost and to adopt programs designed to offend as few people as possible.[6]

As they negotiated a careful path through a minefield of social tensions, educators were also compelled to deal with the effects of a growing civil libertarian critique of schools. Concern about the deadening effects of modern society on the individual, which had been growing since the 1940s, now blossomed into a broad skepticism of all established authority. A growing band of radical social critics exercised a particularly harsh judgment on the school, portraying it as an authoritarian institution that smothered creativity and enforced a dull conformity on unwitting students. Intellectuals such as Paul Goodman, John Holt, Jules Henry, Charles Silberman, Ivan Illich, and Carl Bereiter called for a variety of reforms to provide greater latitude for the young. In most cases their proposals demanded limitations on the school's role in socialization, especially in the realm of moral and political values. For example, Bereiter argued that public schools should teach skills only, leaving the task of moral education to families, churches, and students themselves. "Education in the areas of personality and values," he proclaimed, "is never free of authoritarian imposition." Intrusion of the public school into such personal matters as values was as dangerous as the mingling of church and state.[7]

The proposals of Bereiter and others of his persuasion were extreme, even by the standards of the sixties and seventies, but they moved in the same direction as public opinion. A large number of Americans in these decades came to distrust established institutions, to fear imposition, and to treat values as purely private matters. Some had lost faith in their own ability to manage modern society and were ready to let the young fashion their own values. In this atmosphere, the range of acceptable behavior in such areas as dress, language, and sex expanded enormously, as a kind of pervasive relativism came to apply to a growing number of human activities. Even the majority of parents who refused to demand that schools abandon moral education were increasingly prepared to protest any perceived slight to their own particular values and to side with their children in every dispute with school authorities.

One measure of the effects of social tensions and libertarian pressures in these decades was the enormous increase in litigation involving the schools. As Robert Hampel has pointed out, there were more court cases challenging school practices in the years between 1969 and 1978 than there had been in the entire previous fifty years. Moreover, "the percentage of cases decided in favor of students rose dramatically from 19 percent (before 1969) to 48 percent (1969–1978)."[8] Although court decisions left schools with substantial authority in matters of curriculum and student discipline, educators often misunderstood the careful distinctions of judicial opinions and abandoned even authority that courts had left in their hands. Especially in the areas of values education and student codes of conduct, educators responded to litigation and the threat of litigation by taking safe, defensive positions.

Two areas of judicial activity had especially important consequences for moral education. The first was a series of cases that drew an ever clearer line between church and state in education. A continuation of a long-term trend, the effort to remove religion from the classroom achieved important victories in these decades. The landmark Supreme Court cases came in the 1960s. In *Engel v Vitale* (1962), the Court ruled that a New York program that allowed teachers to begin classes with a nondenominational prayer was unconstitutional. In the *Schempp* case of 1963, the Court ruled against devotional Bible-reading in the public schools, putting an effective end to a practice that had survived many local challenges. Subsequent decisions of federal courts reaffirmed strict barriers between church and state, and efforts to reverse the trend of legal judgments by constitutional amendment failed repeatedly. Although courts explicitly exempted moral education from their prohibitions, many educators of the sixties and seventies saw the trend of judicial decisions as a signal that even purely secular education in the realm of values might violate constitutional standards. As one observer put it, "Many teachers and administrators apparently assumed that since such precepts were bound up with all great religions, they fell under the Supreme Court's prohibitions."[9]

Legal efforts to broaden the rights of children had even more chilling effects on moral education. Often equating the dependency of children with the oppression of other social groups, a number of activists in the 1960s and 1970s sought to broaden the due-process rights of students and curtail the traditional latitude schools had enjoyed in enforcing their codes of behavior. Although courts stopped far short of giving students the same rights of adults, they were intrusive enough to accentuate an already debilitating fear of litigation. Educators increasingly abandoned elaborate codes of conduct that had once provided a powerful tool for moral education and adopted instead only the rules that were essential to school order. Thus, what had once been a way to teach honesty, respect for legitimate authority, and a host of other values now became only a mechanism to enforce a kind of legal minimum of proper behavior.

Moral education, of course, did not disappear altogether in the schools. Many teachers still put a moral point on their lessons, and even the newest textbooks provided a significant sample of the old verities. Some schools continued to provide an ethos in which character was encouraged and moral questions were examined. Moreover, even schools that avoided questions of personal morality often continued to explore the moral dimensions of the great public issues of the day. Yet the trend was in the other direction. Educators avoided controversial moral questions and elevated tolerance into the primary value of the school, in order to create or preserve peace among their competing and often quarreling constituencies. Fearful of charges of imposition, they backed away from anything that might be labelled "indoctrination." Wary and anxious, they lowered their expectations for student behavior and sought to purchase harmony by providing a curriculum broad enough to meet the interests of every conceivable constituency.[10]

What was lost in these decades was not so much the ability of the individual teacher to raise moral issues—determined and skillful people could still manage that. Rather, what was lost was an atmosphere that supported moral education as a primary goal of the school. When particular teachers sought to cultivate character, they worked in the vacuum of an institution that had lost its commitment to the idea. No longer were their efforts systematically supported by the code of student conduct, by the endorsement or acquiescence of parents, by the behavior of the administration, or by the general ethos of the school. More likely, their efforts were scrutinized by interest groups or parents, sanitized by nervous colleagues or principals, or even challenged in the courts.

By the end of the 1970s, moral education had reached a historic low point in the nation's public schools. What had for more than three centuries been a central responsibility of the school had now become both peripheral and problematic. Some critics, such as Gerald Grant, feared that public schools had become so constrained by federal supervision and so bureaucratic in their own organization that they were incapable of creating an ethos to support moral education.[11] Others believed that the decline of moral education had contributed to a significant erosion of the standards of both public and private conduct and warned ominously that the failures of public education might well foretell the failure of civilized society itself. Although many Americans of the 1960s and 1970s witnessed the weakening of moral education with relative equanimity, many others were sufficiently alarmed that they mounted major efforts either to restore what had been lost or to create entirely new schemes to provide moral instruction to the nation's young.

The Quest for Revival, 1965–Present

Even as schools seemed to move inexorably away from moral education and educational leaders focused increasingly on other agendas, a handful of prominent intellectuals together with a large number of ordinary Americans sought to spark a revival of interest in matters of character and conduct. Representing a range of disparate groups, these Americans worked along independent, sometimes competing, lines to restore moral education of one kind or another to the nation's public schools. Although some people had resisted the decline of moral education throughout the postwar era, the efforts to spark a revival gained an important place in educational discourse only in the mid-1960s, when some theorists began to develop entirely new approaches to moral education and others began an aggressive campaign to restore older schemes to their once-lofty place in the public school. These reformers worked against the tide of events in the 1960s and 1970s, but some of them began to have a substantial impact in the 1980s and 1990s, suggesting that the fate of moral education in the schools had not yet been finally sealed.

Three dramatically new approaches to moral education emerged in the years between the mid-1960s and the late 1990s: values clarification, cognitive developmentalism, and a feminist approach that emphasized an ethic of caring. Proponents of all three approaches found traditional virtue-centered moral education to be at best incomplete and at worst a threat to individual freedom. In the spirit of the day, all three approaches were consistent with contemporary American commitments to personal autonomy and the diversity of cultures and lifestyles.

Values Clarification

Of these three new approaches to moral education, values clarification had the earliest impact on educational practice. Developed first by Louis E. Raths, Merrill Harmin, and Sydney B. Simon, who published their volume *Values and Teaching* in 1966, and modified later by Howard Kirschenbaum and others, values clarification offered a clear, comprehensible, and immediately appealing program, especially to those who had grown weary of traditional approaches.[12] Because its developers provided a wealth of instructional materials and pedagogical advice, values clarification was easily transported into the schools. A wide variety of teachers, but especially those in the social studies, added the values clarification exercises to their courses, and the program spread rapidly throughout the late sixties and early seventies.

Like the progressives, values clarificationists were impressed by the situational character of moral decision-making. They denied that any one set of values could possibly obtain at all times and in all places. In a world of constant change, children needed to learn not a set of fixed values but rather a process of valuing. This was especially the case in the contemporary era, when the pace of change seemed to increase exponentially and the range of options open to the young was wider than it had ever been before. What made the matter especially pressing to these reformers was their sense that the troubles of youth in modern America stemmed not from emotional disturbances but rather from the difficulty of choosing values. Drawing heavily on the widespread concern in the early sixties about inability of individuals to develop feelings of authenticity and commitment, the proponents of values clarification sought to help the young find a sense of direction in their personal values and develop a relationship with the society that was *"positive, purposeful, enthusiastic, proud."*[13]

Values clarificationists emphasized the personal and individual nature of valuing, especially in their earliest formulations. In their view, the modern world offered an extraordinary variety of values from which to choose, and like a consumer in the supermarket, "each person has to wrest his own values from the available array."[14] "Could it be, we wonder," Raths, Harmin, and Simon asked rhetorically, "that the pace and complexity of modern life has so exacerbated the problem of deciding what is good and what is right and what is worthy and what is desirable that large numbers of children are finding it increasingly bewildering, even overwhelming, to decide what is worth valuing, what is worth one's time and energy?" The question defined the premise that underlay their whole scheme: that children needed to learn a process of choosing values that would provide them with a sense of purpose in a world perplexingly full of options.[15]

To help the bewildered young find their way, values clarificationists proposed that teachers use nonindoctrinative and nonjudgmental methods to help students discover and refine their values. They neither prescribed the values to be taught nor even insisted on the teaching of "moral" values; instead, they defined values as preferences in all realms of life. The teacher was to stimulate thought and to encourage a process of valuing that, in the scheme of Raths, Harmin, and Simon, involved choosing freely, choosing from among alternatives, choosing after thoughtful consideration of the consequences of each alternative, prizing and cherishing, acting upon choices, and repeating the actions.[16]

To help teachers in this task, the early leaders of the values clarification movement and many of their disciples offered a rich set of materials and a wealth of practical advice. They proposed three specific approaches to the task of values clarification: dialogue, in which teachers asked questions of individual students to help them clarify their values; value sheets, written statements describing dilemmas or situations followed by questions to be answered privately by students; and group discussions, which might be organized around pictures without captions, stories, or scenes from a current movie. Guidebooks for teachers offered detailed advice for every strategy: lists of clarifying questions, problems and questions for value sheets, and an array of exercises for group discussion.

In all of these activities teachers were expected to avoid imposing their own values on students. Where honesty and openness compelled them to reveal their views, teachers were to make clear that their values were personal and might not be desirable for others. As Raths et al. sternly put it to the teachers: "We all have different experiences and outlooks, and we should all select values that are individually suitable." The primary function of teachers was not to dwell on their own values but rather to elicit the views of students and to respond to them without "moralizing, criticizing, giving values, or evaluating. The adult excludes all hints of 'good' or 'right' or 'acceptable' or their opposites." The atmosphere was to be "permissive and stimulating, but not insistent."[17] Although supporters of values clarification resisted the analogy, the role of the teacher in their scheme closely resembled the role of the humane therapist dealing with a client struggling to find a personal path in a bewildering world.[18]

Despite the appeal of such a nondirective approach, values clarification engendered harsh criticism from the outset. The most persistent charge was that it encouraged ethical relativism. Critics charged that by focusing on the process of valuing and by uncritically validating individual preferences, values clarification muddied the difference between moral principles and personal preferences and encouraged students to think that all moral positions were equally valid. "Values clarification," declared philosopher Kenneth A. Strike, "makes all moral principles into values and values into matters of personal preference. Its having done so, the enforcement of any value can only be an act of arbitrary will."[19] The danger was that students emerged from the process with no sense of how to deal with moral conflict or establish moral priorities. A sense of authenticity or commitment was no substitute for the ability to make difficult moral decisions.

Not all critics were convinced that values clarification was itself entirely value-free. Some found in the scheme dangerous possibilities for invasion of privacy, emotional manipulation, and even moral indoctrination. They were skeptical that schools could be entirely neutral and feared that unsuspecting students would be led to accept the biases of teachers or peers. The subtlety of the methods only enhanced the possibility of effective imposition. Moreover, some of the materials distributed by values clarificationists seemed to be far from free of political bias. One critic, William Casement, provided an example: "In an exercise entitled 'What one person can do,' students are instructed to list 'ten things they can do for the environment.' Built into the exercise, because of the way it is worded, is a bias in favor of environmental preservation. This value must be accepted before one makes the list. Students who participate in the exercise are being subtly led to accept a specific content."[20]

The gentlest criticism of the new scheme was articulated best by philosopher Andrew Oldenquist, who suggested that beneath the surface relativism of the values clarificationists lay a romantic faith that "people will be naturally kind, honest, fair, diligent, and so on, if only they are stroked well and are not corrupted or psychologically damaged in some way." Perhaps, Oldenquist surmised, this faith explains why their approach resembled modern psychotherapy. Because they believed that people were "naturally good—as it were, naturally civilized—they believed that moral education, as most people understand the notion, is unnecessary: the wants and preference that they 'clarify' will be good ones—that is, kind, honest, fair, and considerate."[21]

Whatever the presuppositions of the values clarificationists, the scheme's relativistic methods made it an easy target for a variety of critics ranging from moral philosophers to religious fundamentalists. To many Americans, already disturbed by the moral laxity of day, values clarification seemed less a remedy for than an extension of the problem. Under a barrage of criticism, the scheme lost its hold in the late seventies almost as quickly as it had burst onto the scene in the mid-sixties. Even at its high point the popularity of values clarification had depended largely on the enthusiasm of particular teachers who had simply added it to existing classroom activities instead of finding it a secure place in a reformed curriculum. When criticism grew, enthusiasm quickly waned, and the scheme lost its influence on American education.

Cognitive Developmentalism

At the same time that values clarificationists were elaborating their program, other theorists were exploring an approach that emphasized the development of moral reasoning or judgment. Working along parallel lines, a number of philosophers, psychologists, and educators sought to find a way to refine moral judgment without teaching a specific set of values. Of these theorists Lawrence A. Kohlberg, a Harvard psychologist, won by far the greatest following. His theories of cognitive moral development were bold and conceptually rich, and his work quickly captured the imagination of many intellectuals and educational leaders. From the mid-1960s, when his ideas first became widely known, until the present, Kohlberg's theories have occupied a central place in the discourse about moral education.

Kohlberg's theories are far more difficult to characterize than are the doctrines of values clarification, because they changed in significant ways over the years. A restless thinker and active reformer, Kohlberg modified his proposals frequently in response both to criticism and to practical experience with his system. Yet despite the constant evolution of his ideas, it is possible to identify roughly two stages in his thought: an early stage, in which he emphasized a fairly narrow cognitive approach to moral education; and a later stage, in which he endorsed a much more comprehensive approach.

The early Kohlberg shared some of the preconceptions of the values clarificationists. He feared indoctrination and was more interested in the process of moral decision-making than in the content of moral values. Moreover, he joined in condemning traditional efforts to teach specific values, contemptuously dismissing them as misguided attempts to pawn off on children someone else's "bag of virtues."[22] Yet Kohlberg had a far more tightly constructed system than values clarificationists, and his scheme focused more narrowly on the purely cognitive dimensions of moral growth. Thus, despite certain common attitudes toward traditional practices, Kohlberg and the clarificationists were competitors rather than collaborators on most issues surrounding moral education in the years after 1965.

Kohlberg's early theories grew out of his doctoral work at the University of Chicago in the late 1950s and owed much to the thought of both John Dewey and Jean Piaget. Fascinated by the notion that moral reasoning progressed through identifiable stages, he used his dissertation to explore the response of youths to certain moral dilemmas. On the basis of this study he posited the existence of six stages of cognitive moral development and in subsequent work concluded that classroom activities could encourage children to advance more quickly to higher stages of reasoning.[23] By the mid-1960s Kohlberg had developed a comprehensive conception of cognitive moral development, and his theories began to attract the interest of a broad range of educators.

The key to Kohlberg's early theories was his notion that children moved in orderly ways through stages of moral reasoning. He posited the existence of six stages grouped in three general levels:

LEVEL I—PREMORAL

Stage 1. Obedience and punishment orientation. Egocentric deference to superior power or prestige, or a trouble-avoiding set. Objective responsibility.
Stage 2. Naively egoistic orientation. Right action is that instrumentally satisfying the self's needs and occasionally other's. Awareness of relativism of value to each actor's needs and perspective. Naive egalitarianism and orientation to exchange and reciprocity.

LEVEL II—CONVENTIONAL ROLE CONFORMITY

Stage 3. Good-boy orientation. Orientation to approval and to pleasing others. Conformity to stereotypical images of majority or natural role behavior, and judgment of intentions.

Stage 4. Authority and social-order-maintaining orientation. Orientation to 'doing duty' and to showing respect for authority and maintaining the given social order for its own sake. Regard for earned expectations of others.

LEVEL III—SELF-ACCEPTED MORAL PRINCIPLES

Stage 5. Contractual legalistic orientation. Recognition of an arbitrary element or starting point in rules or expectations for the sake of agreement. Duty defined in terms of contract, general avoidance of violation of the will or rights of others, and majority will and welfare.

Stage 6. Conscience or principle orientation. Orientation not only to actually ordained social rules but to principles of choice involving appeal to logical universality and consistency. Orientation to conscience as a directing agent and to mutual respect and trust.[24]

Although Kohlberg refined these stages at several later times in order to clarify them or to respond to critics, the notion of discrete stages leading from a relatively primitive, selfish orientation to a universalistic and principled position survived all of his revisions.

Kohlberg's research in Chicago and in various cross-cultural settings convinced him of the universality of moral growth through identifiable stages. He argued: (1) that more than half of any individual's thinking was "at one stage with the remainder at the next adjacent stages (which he or she is leaving or is moving into)"; (2) that people always moved sequentially from one level to another without ever skipping a stage; and (3) that people rarely regressed. Thus, in attempting to encourage moral growth, educators were working in harmony with a natural tendency of people in all cultures to move upward from lower to higher stages of reasoning. Although few people reached the highest stage, Kohlberg was convinced that some growth could be achieved in almost everyone.[25]

Kohlberg's early pedagogy reflected his understanding of the stages of moral reasoning and his commitment to the importance of the cognitive dimensions of moral growth. At the core of his method was his belief that students grew through cognitive conflict, especially through argument with students at the next higher stage of development. Such conflict, he believed, created a "sense of disequilibrium about one's own position" and led students to see the advantages of the higher-level approaches. The role of the teacher in this scheme was to provoke the appropriate discussion, often raising probing questions of his or her own in the process. Kohlberg's favorite technique for eliciting the debate was the presentation of hard-case ethical dilemmas. Students were expected to resolve the dilemmas and defend their positions. Teachers gauged the progress of students not by the solutions they developed—the dilemmas could be resolved in a number of ways—but rather by the quality of moral reasoning they used in arriving at their final positions.

By emphasizing the process of moral reasoning rather than the teaching of specific virtues, Kohlberg hoped to avoid the charge of indoctrination. His scheme, he argued, was nonindoctrinative in both purpose and method. "First," he wrote, "it is non-indoctrinative because it is not addressed to transmitting specific value-content but to stimulating a new way of thinking and judging. Second, it is non-indoctrinative because it is not imposing something alien on the student. Movement to the next stage is movement in a direction natural to him, it is movement in the only direction he can go." Procedurally the approach was nonindoctrinative because teachers stirred debate and asked questions without ever attempting to impose their own values.[26]

Despite his effort to develop a nonindoctrinative approach to moral education, Kohlberg's system was hardly value-free. His definition of stages and his assumption that higher stages were better than lower stages revealed a clear commitment to a principle of justice. Although that commitment was in Kohlberg's thought from the beginning, he talked about it more freely as concern about indoctrination declined in the 1970s. The principle of justice that informed the highest stages of reasoning, Kohlberg declared in 1975, was drawn from the "liberal or rational tradition running from Kant through Mill and Dewey to John Rawls. Central to this tradition is the claim that an adequate morality is *principled*, that is, that it makes judgments in terms of *universal* principles applicable to all people. *Principles* are to be distinguished from *rules*. Conventional morality is grounded on rules, primarily 'thou shalt nots' such as are represented by the Ten Commandments. Rules are prescriptions of kinds of actions; principles are, rather, universal guides to making a moral decision."[27]

Even after he had clarified his commitment to a principle of justice, however, Kohlberg left open the questions of the connection between moral reasoning and moral action. In response to critics who warned that moral behavior required more than high-level reasoning skills, Kohlberg admitted that "one can reason in terms of principles and not live up to these principles." Yet he was convinced that mature moral judgement was a necessary condition for mature moral action. "Moral judgment," he declared, "while only one factor in moral behavior, is the single most important or influential factor yet discovered in moral behavior."[28] By stimulating higher levels of moral reasoning, the school did not guarantee better behavior; but in Kohlberg's view, it made a significant contribution to that end.

Despite Kohlberg's claims about the connections between moral reasoning and moral action, it was the narrow focus on cognitive development that engendered the harshest criticism of Kohlberg's early theories. Skeptics argued that dealing with hard cases represented only a small part of moral conduct and that students needed both to learn more concrete principles and to acquire good moral habits. They feared that the heavy emphasis on moral discussion neglected the problem of motivation and led to a kind of rhetorical sophistication that gave students the ability to rationalize their actions without inspiring them to behave in principled ways. "It is questionable," declared critic Kevin Ryan, "whether American parents are going to buy an approach to moral education that concentrates exclusively on thinking and has so little to say about how children actually behave. My own concern is the turning of this whole issue of moral education into a word game with few implications for action. Teaching our children how to discourse about complex personal and social issues without helping them in the world of action could be an empty and dangerous victory."[29]

The charge of narrowness struck a responsive chord in Kohlberg, especially as he became more involved in actual educational reform in the 1970s and 1980s. Working in both prisons and troubled schools, Kohlberg came to appreciate the need for moral instruction that went well beyond discussion of dilemmas. "I realize now," wrote Kohlberg in 1978, "that the psychologists's abstraction of moral 'cognition' (judgment and reasoning) from moral action, and the abstraction of structure in moral cognition and judgment from content are necessary abstractions for certain psychological research purposes. It is not a sufficient guide to the moral educator who deals with the moral concrete in a school world in which value content as well as structure, behavior as well as reasoning, must be dealt with. In this context, the educator must be a socializer teaching value content and behavior, and not only a Socratic or Rogerian process-facilitator of development."[30]

Having accepted the need for a more comprehensive moral education than his early scheme provided, Kohlberg proposed a dramatic reform—the creation of "just community schools," schools that operated as democratic communities with students sharing fully in the establishing and enforcing of codes of conduct. Reminiscent of progressive experiments, the just community school sought to use the culture and climate of the school to encourage moral growth. Instead of discussing mythical dilemmas chosen for their complexity and difficulty, students in the new schools wrestled with the immediate problems of the community itself. Indoctrination, Kohlberg acknowledged, was inevitable in such a scheme, but he no longer feared indoctrination in a democratic setting. "I now believe," he wrote, "that moral education can be in the form of advocacy or 'indoctrination' without violating the child's rights if there is an explicit recognition of shared rights of teachers and students and as long as teacher advocacy is democratic, or subject to the constraints of recognizing student participation in the rule-making and value-upholding process."[31]

Although the abrupt reversal represented by the just community school quieted critics who had charged Kohlberg with narrowness, it provided additional ammunition for those who accused him of liberal bias. The suspicion that Kohlberg had an agenda akin to the elite liberalism of the 1960s was an old one. "Kohlberg's *Hypothetical Dilemmas for Use in the Classroom*," wrote Andrew Oldenquist, "is simply packed with moral content that flows from his ideals of liberalism, participatory democracy, sexual freedom, and children's rights."[32] The just community school, with all of its neoprogressive trappings, seemed designed to promote those values in an even more compelling way, as conservative critics were eager to point out.

The fate of Kohlberg's ideas—both old and new—is far from clear. Although the use of moral dilemmas has never been a common practice in schools, the idea has not entirely lost its appeal, even in the face of Kohlberg's own declaration of its limitations. Some prominent figures in social studies education, for example, have found promise in Kohlberg's early pedagogy and have tried to make a place for the use of dilemmas in citizenship education. The just community school has also attracted attention, and with the help of a devoted band of Kohlberg disciples, a number of cities have established just community schools of their own. Yet neither reform has yet had a broad effect on educational practice. Although it is clear that Kohlberg's theories have been more enduring than those of the values clarificationists, it is not yet clear that they will have a lasting impact on educational practice.

Feminist Approaches: The Role of Caring

Debate about narrowness and liberal bias dominated discussion of Kohlberg's ideas, especially in the 1960s and 1970s; but in the 1980s several feminist writers raised another concern—namely, that Kohlberg's emphasis on justice and rights had a masculine bias to it. Noting that women seemed not to score as well as men on Kohlberg's scale of moral development, they argued that Kohlberg's system failed to take into account the fact that women went about the process of moral reasoning in a substantially different way. Carol Gilligan, Kohlberg's colleague and most astute feminist critic, believed that women differ from men in several ways: (1) they tend to pay more attention to the effect of actions on relationships; (2) they tend to be more interested in the context of moral decisions; (3) they tend to be more concerned about the resolution of real rather than hypothetical dilemmas; and (4) they are more likely to tie moral judgments to feelings of empathy and compassion.[33]

Gilligan believed that the moral development of women could best be understood as a three-stage growth of caring. "In this sequence," she wrote,

> an initial focus on caring for the self in order to ensure survival is followed by a transitional phase in which this judgment is criticized as selfish. The criticism signals a new understanding of the connection between self and others which is articulated by the concept of responsibility. The elaboration of this concept of responsibility and its fusion with a maternal morality that seeks to ensure care for the dependent and unequal characterizes the second perspective. . . . The third perspective focuses on the dynamics of relationships and dissipates the tension between selfishness and responsibility through a new understanding of the interconnection between other and self. Care becomes the self-chosen principle of a judgment that remains psychological in its concern with relationships and response but becomes universal in its condemnation of exploitation and hurt.[34]

Gilligan's work, along with that of Nel Noddings, Jane Roland Martin, and others, stirred a quest for an entirely new approach to moral education, one that would take into account the emotional component of moral growth and make a central place for an ethic of caring. Such a program, Noddings argued, would balance the voice of the father, who speaks the language of rights, with the voice of the mother, who uses the language of caring and compassion, and provide a program that would promote the moral growth of men and women alike.[35]

Although feminists have yet to develop the kinds of educational materials that their rival theorists have produced, they have articulated a vision of a classroom in which caring relationships lie at the core of moral education. Using the intimate relations of domestic life as a model, Noddings has argued for a schooling in which children are provided with "practice in caring." "Children," she wrote, "can work together formally and informally on a host of school projects, and, as they get older, they can help younger children, contribute to the care of buildings and grounds, and eventually—under careful supervision—do volunteer work in the community."[36]

In a scheme somewhat reminiscent of the expanding-horizons approach to the social studies promoted by progressives in the 1930s, Noddings proposed a thorough reorganization of the curriculum around the theme of caring: "We would like to give a central place to the questions and issues that lie at the core of human existence. One possibility would be to organize the curriculum around themes of care—caring for self, for intimate others, for strangers and global others, for the natural world and its nonhuman creatures, for the human-made world, and for ideas."[37]

Despite their critique of the cognitive developmentalists, feminists have remained closer to progressive and Kohlbergian traditions than to virtue-centered approaches. The classrooms they envisioned share important elements with both progressive and just community schools. Moreover, feminists have frequently made common cause with proponents of other neoprogressive movements in education, including social learning, constructivism, and social reconstructionism. Although tensions remain between them and the cognitive developmentalists, feminists have in the 1990s played a primary role in defining an approach to moral education that remains in the progressive tradition.

Character Education: In Defense of the Virtues

The novelty of values clarification, cognitive developmentalism, and feminist approaches have given them a special place in educational discourse in the years since the mid-1960s, but the most broad-based efforts to revitalize moral education have come from a variety of groups and individuals who favored traditional, virtue-centered approaches, now labelled "character education" to distinguish them from their contemporary competitors. In the style of programs that had once dominated American classrooms, character education emphasized the teaching of specific virtues and the cultivation of good conduct. Although its proponents were not unconcerned with the processes of valuing and moral reasoning, they were far more interested in content than in process.

The defense of character education was remarkable for its breadth and vigor. It was led by two loose collections of supporters: the somewhat marginal constituencies who had defended virtue-centered education since the 1930s, when it had begun to lose its hold; and a newly alarmed group of elite intellectuals and educational leaders. Disturbed by both the erosion of moral education and by what they perceived to be dangers in values clarification and cognitive-developmental schemes, these groups mounted the strongest campaign for virtue-centered education the nation had witnessed since the early twentieth century.

The two groups of supporters rarely acted in concert; rather, they worked along parallel lines, bringing different strengths and different perspectives to the common cause of reviving character education. The first group continued an effort that had been carried out before by the likes of Henry Lester Smith and Ernest Ligon, who had fought a long string of battles against progressivism and other forces that threatened to remove virtue-centered moral education from the schools. The effective headquarters for this campaign after the mid-1960s was the American Institute of Character Education (AICE), located in San Antonio, Texas. Heavily financed by private foundations—including that long-time supporter of character education, the Lilly Endowment—AICE operated largely outside mainstream educational circles, but it managed to have a significant effect on many public schools over the years.

The primary activity of AICE was "to write a practical, useful, and workable program to teach the essential traits of character, conduct, and citizenship to the elementary students of our public school system." Like many of the early twentieth-century character-education programs, it was organized around a code, called "Freedom's Code" in this case, which extolled the familiar virtues: being honest, generous, just, kind, and helpful; having courage and convictions along with tolerance of the views of others; making good use of time and talents; providing security for self and dependents; understanding and fulfilling the obligations of citizenship; standing for truth; and defending basic human rights under a government of law.[38]

Prepared first in the late 1960s and revised in the 1970s, AICE's Character Education Curriculum was designed for grades K through 6. Provided to schools in kits, the materials included books, filmstrips, story wheels, transparencies, and teachers' manuals. The books differed from standard readers only in their careful and explicit focus on the teaching of virtues. Although they were designed to be used as a part of language arts or social studies courses, if teachers preferred, the authors of the curriculum favored separate time periods for character education: five to ten minutes each day in kindergarten, longer periods for higher grades. Teachers were expected to use a variety of pedagogical techniques—discussion, stories, role playing, projects, case studies, and the like—and to encourage students throughout the school day to practice the virtues they had learned.[39]

Although the Character Education Curriculum attracted relatively little attention in established educational forums, it spread rapidly in elementary schools, reaching as many as eighteen thousand classrooms in forty-four states by the late 1980s.[40] Its effectiveness has been a matter of dispute. Supporters have claimed that it has reduced alcohol and drug abuse, encouraged school attendance, and helped combat vandalism. Skeptics have wondered whether any program that occupied only a few minutes of the school day could have had a substantial impact. Whatever the final resolution of that debate, it seems clear that the Character Education Curriculum has provided elementary school materials on moral education not easily available from other late twentieth-century sources. At the same time, it is questionable whether the materials are extensive enough to restore moral education to a central place in the life of the school.

For the most part, AICE and its supporters have chosen not to participate directly in the modern debate on moral education. Instead they have
worked quietly, spreading their traditional gospel through new materials
and dealing with teachers and principals directly rather than through the
nation's great educational associations. The other group of character education supporters, however, have been lively participants in the contemporary clashes. Indeed, the formidable challenges of the values clarificationists, the Kohlbergians, and, to a lesser degree, the feminists have done
much to spur them to action, and they have responded with a searching
critique of modern theories and a vigorous, sophisticated defense of virtue-
centered character education.

More a cluster of like-minded individuals than a collection of people
with direct links to each other, the elite supporters of character education
ranged from intellectuals in universities and think tanks to powerful educational leaders. Many, though not all, shared a political and pedagogical
conservatism, and their efforts bore greatest fruit in the 1980s and 1990s
when the cultural climate was friendlier than it had been in the 1960s and
1970s. Indeed, in some senses most were involved in an educational coun-
terrevolution, seeking to restore both academic and behavioral standards
they believed had been destroyed by the disruptions of the sixties and seventies. Among the most powerful and articulate of the group were William J. Bennett, director of the National Endowment for the Humanities in
the early Reagan years, then secretary of the U.S. Department of Education; Bill Honig, superintendent of public instruction in California; and
university professors Andrew Oldenquist, Kevin Ryan, James Wilson, and
Edward Wynne. By any measure Bennett was the most influential, using
his high positions in government as a pulpit from which to preach the need
for a revival in character education.

These elite supporters of character education were appalled by the
growing "amorality" of the school and blamed it in part for the soaring
rates of social pathology among youth in the modern era. They pointed to
alarming rates of teenage suicide, crime, drug use, and unwed pregnan-
cies and called for a renewed commitment to moral education. The school,
they charged, had done much to encourage toleration and to enhance the
rights of minorities, but it had said little or nothing about "individual ethical responsibilities—why we should not murder, rape, assault, or rob our
fellow citizens."[41] If schools failed to provide more guidance, they worried, children would look "for group values elsewhere, in the sentimental
and violent world of television or in the tumultuous and ethically confused
world of their peers."[42]

From their perspective, none of the new approaches to moral education offered effective remedies. They were particularly critical of values

clarification and cognitive developmentalism, which they judged to be narrow and incomplete at best and dangerous at worst. Bennett and others believed that discussion of moral dilemmas might have a place in the high school but argued that a complete character education required much more than study of hard cases. They were even more wary of values clarification, fearing that it would deepen an already dangerous relativism in the society. What was needed, then, was nothing short of a return to virtue-centered character education. "Moral education without justified moral content is most likely to be perceived as a pointless game," wrote Oldenquist. "What we owe to children is strong direction in the actual acquisition of morality, not just chatter about morality."[43] This meant moral education with an emphasis on the virtues and a parallel concern with behavior. It also meant the use of directive as well as nondirective methods of teaching the appropriate values.

The elite supporters of character education did not share the widespread anxieties about imposition that had made moral education so difficult in the 1960s and 1970s. They were convinced that most basic moral values would create little controversy. "The vast majority of us would agree," wrote Honig, "that a good person is generous to others, not miserly or self-absorbed; modestly self-assured, not vain or boastful; faithful, not promiscuous; prudent, not rash or prodigal; reverent to the elderly, not brusque or insolent; optimistic, not envious; forgiving, not vengeful; hospitable, discrete, loving, patient, not hostile, overbearing, cold, or slapdash."[44] The task of finding a wide consensus on fundamental values was not that difficult, argued Bennett, and the time had come to "demystify" the subject and "get down to business."[45]

Bennett, Honig, and others proposed a comprehensive approach to character education, one that began in the early years and continued through college. Like their predecessors in the nineteenth and early twentieth century, they believed that possibilities for moral education lay in every part of the curriculum. "We don't have to reinvent the wheel," wrote Bennett, "And we don't have to add new courses. We have a wealth of material to draw on—material that virtually all schools once taught to students for the sake of shaping character. And this is material that we can teach in our regular courses, in our English and history courses."[46] Stories offered a particularly rich source of moral instruction, as Bennett sought to demonstrate in his immensely popular *Book of Virtues*, a collection of classic tales designed to teach such values as honesty and compassion. The stories enabled teachers to discuss ethical questions and connected students to the culture and traditions that provided them their moral moorings.[47]

The clarion call of these reformers was not for a new pedagogy but rather for a return to an older tradition of moral education. Unlike the Kohlbergians and other modern reformers, they sought to emphasize the basic virtues and common values and to avoid the controversial issues of the day. "The formation of character in young people," declared Bennett, "is educationally a different task, and a prior task to the discussion of the great, difficult, controversial disputes of the day. . . . You have to walk before you can run, and you ought to be able to run straight before you are asked to run an obstacle course or a mine field. So the moral basics should be taught first. The tough issues can, if teachers and parents wish, be taken up later."[48] Similarly, political squabbles had no place in the classroom. Both the left and the right, wrote Honig, had been guilty of undue intrusion in the classroom. "Children should not be taught that all those who oppose the nuclear freeze are warmongers, nor that all those who favor a woman's right to an abortion are murderers."[49]

By taking an aggressive stance on both the teaching of specific virtues and the use of directive pedagogies, the elite supporters of character education opened themselves to the same criticisms that were leveled against their early twentieth-century counterparts. Some critics quickly questioned the effectiveness of the approach, harkening back to the Hartshorne and May studies to support their case. The greatest challenge, however, has come on the issue of indoctrination. Not only have critics charged that the scheme promotes conventional morality, but they have raised suspicions about what they perceive to be a conservative political and educational bias that is insufficiently sensitive to the diversity of the society. Kohlbergians have been particularly skeptical. Even though their most recent experiments have embraced some teaching of virtues, they have been careful to contrast the effects of indoctrination in traditional classrooms with the consequences of indoctrination in the democratic settings of the just community school.

Of all the modern movements in moral education, the effect of the effort to restore character education to the schools is the most difficult to measure. Although the use of the materials of AICE provides one index of the effect of the Character Education Curriculum, scholars have yet to find a way to measure the impact of the elite campaign for character education. Every evidence suggests that public school leaders, perhaps emboldened by Bennett and other powerful figures, have become less skittish about moral education—but it is not yet clear that textbooks have been altered to reflect the new emphasis or that teachers have begun to talk about moral issues in the way that their pre-1960 predecessors had done.

Private Alternatives

The vast majority of Americans who worked to revive moral education after 1965 focused their efforts on the public school. Despite the disheartening developments of the 1960s and 1970s, they still believed that reform was possible within the traditional framework of public education. Many others, however, were convinced that the situation in public schools had deteriorated to the point that character education had become an impossibility. Pessimistic about the prospect of reversing the trend, they began to turn to private education, holding out the hope that in this more guarded atmosphere questions of character would receive the attention they deserved.

Interest in private education emerged from a variety of quarters, and it led to expanding enrollments in every kind of private schooling except Roman Catholic schools. Between 1965 and 1989, enrollment in nonreligious independent schools rose from 199,454 to 915,106, a gain of 358 percent, while enrollment in non-Catholic religious schools rose from 595,999 to 1,864,757, an increase of 213 percent.[50] Not all of this growth is attributable to concern about moral education, since many parents were equally disturbed by declining academic standards in public schools; but a widespread belief in the ability of private education to shape character figured prominently in the new stature of independent and religious schools.

Independent Schools

Scholars have yet to give systematic study to the growth of nonreligious independent schools, but impressionistic evidence suggests that their reputed superiority in developing character played a significant role in their new popularity. Many of those most distressed about the decline of moral education in public schools pointed with envy to the record of private institutions, where character development was often a primary goal. Because independent schools were less subject to judicial scrutiny and bureaucratic intrusion and because they usually served a less diverse clientele, they had a freer hand in offering courses in religion and ethics and in exercising a careful supervision of student behavior. Especially in elite boarding schools, teachers and administrators were able to set a moral tone that pervaded every facet of school life. For parents who could afford to send their children to them, the climate of private schools provided an alluring alternative to a troubled public system.[51]

The Christian Day School

The importance of moral education is even clearer in the case of religious schools. Sponsors and parents alike openly expressed their disillusionment with the state of moral education in public schools and established character development as an overriding purpose of their private systems. Thus, the growth in Jewish and Protestant private education roughly paralleled the decline in the moral climate of public schools. Some of the expansion took place in established systems, such as those sponsored by Lutherans, Orthodox Jews, and Mennonites, but the major engine of growth was the creation of Christian day schools by evangelical and fundamentalist Protestants. A nondenominational and largely uncoordinated effort, this movement drew its strongest support from Southern Baptists, Free Will Methodists, Assemblies of God, Nazarines, the Brethren, American Baptists, and a variety of smaller sects and independent congregations.[52]

Before the 1960s, these groups had generally supported public education. Even as their influence waned in the first half of the twentieth century, they chose not leave the public school but rather to concentrate their energies on retaining a place for religion and moral education. As they won fewer and fewer battles in the 1950s and 1960s, however, many of them finally gave up on public education and turned instead to a solution they had previously condemned—the creation of private religious schools. Although the diffuse character of their movement makes precise figures difficult, the best students of the phenomenon estimate that by 1965 more than 110,000 students attended Christian day schools. By 1989, the number of schools had reached 7,851 (just short of the number of Catholic schools) and enrollments had grown to more than 985,000.[53]

Evangelicals and fundamentalists cited both religious and moral concerns as reasons for turning away from the public school. The elimination of prayer, Bible-reading, and other religious exercises from the classroom, along with the teaching of evolution and moral relativism, led them to argue that the public school had elevated secular humanism into an established religion of its own. "For over twenty-five years," wrote evangelist Tim LaHaye, "I have been watching the California school system, in which every evil fad conjured up by the humanists has been instituted. When my daughter was in the ninth grade and my son was in the seventh, I began doing battle with the humanists in our local junior high. Many of the moral convictions and standards I taught my children were ridiculed, and they were subjected to humiliation and scorn by their peers. The vice-principal of that school, a committed humanist, determined to undermine the training of my children against my will."[54]

LaHaye and others of his persuasion traced the influence of secular humanism to John Dewey, and they were especially critical of anything in education that smacked of progressivism. "Protestant influence on public education," declared Paul A. Kienel, executive director of the California Association of Christian Schools, "lost much of its grip during the late '20s and early '30s. During this period, Columbia University became known for its teachers college and for the man who headed the college, philosopher and educator John Dewey, the father of U.S. progressive education. He was a member of the board of the American Humanist Association in

1933—the year it hammered out the first Humanist Manifesto which said that 'faith in the prayer-hearing God . . . is an unproved and outmoded faith.'" Progressive reform, in this view, had initiated a process that eventually rooted out all Christianity from the schools and established in its place a purely secular worldview as the religion of public education.[55]

As much as evangelicals and fundamentalists complained about the secularism of public schools, social-scientific studies revealed that parents who sent children to Christian day schools were much more likely to be influenced by the moral tone of public education than by its neglect of religion.[56] The weakening of discipline, the spread of drugs, and the pervasive relativism encouraged them to seek a safer haven for their young, a place where the lessons would "not be at cross purposes with the teachings of the home and the church."[57] The Christian day school was for these parents a refuge from both a culture and an educational system that seemed to assault their values on every front.

Although Christian day schools took a variety of forms, most of them infused every facet of the day's activities with religious and moral content. Prayer, Bible-reading, spiritual counseling, and careful supervision of conduct were a central part of every Christian day school, although the tone and intensity varied enormously from place to place. Most schools offered a relatively simple curriculum that focused more on the building of character than on preparation for specific vocations, and most hired teachers less for their pedagogical training than for their religious faith and moral stature. Teachers and principals worked closely with families and churches to insure a comprehensive and well-coordinated effort to achieve the goal of educating morally upright and doctrinally sound Christian men and women.[58]

The task of finding appropriate classroom materials was initially a formidable one for Christian schools. Some adopted public school textbooks and left teachers with the task of placing lessons in a Christian context. Others put together materials of their own, sometimes at great expense. The majority of Christian day schools, however, adopted the Accelerated Christian Education program (ACE), a comprehensive scheme that provided schools with virtually every kind of material or service they required, including curricula and learning materials for grades K-12, instructors' manuals, testing kits, furniture, and even a week of training for principals and teachers. Developed and sold by a for-profit corporation in Garland, Texas, ACE made it possible for even small groups of the faithful to establish schools quickly and inexpensively. The scheme emphasized individual learning and provided packets (called PACEs) for students to work through at their own speed. Teachers moved from desk to desk helping students with the highly structured exercises, then at the appropriate time gave each of them a final examination.

The ACE curriculum was a narrow one that emphasized the basic academic subjects and offered little room for choice of studies. The individual learning packets used virtually every lesson as an opportunity to mingle the moral and spiritual with the academic. Like the primers of colonial America, they quoted scripture freely and infused even the lessons in reading and mathematics with moral meaning. Rigidly ideological, the ACE materials promoted patriotism and social conservatism; condemned socialism, liberalism, and humanism; and even hinted strongly that Catholics and Jews were morally inferior. Students who completed twelve years of the ACE curriculum took with them a solid foundation in basic skills (graduates tended to score well on standardized tests) and a thorough grounding in conservative evangelical or fundamentalist values.

The Decline of Catholic Schooling

As enthusiasm for Christian day schools and other forms of Protestant and Jewish private education grew, many people who had once championed public schools now found themselves taking positions that had initially been staked out by nineteenth-century American Catholics. Ironically, at precisely the same time, a growing number of Catholics were moving in the opposite direction, abandoning parochial schools and sending their children to public schools. Enrollment in Catholic parochial schools, which reached a peak of 5,662,328 in 1964 plummeted to 2,551,119 in 1989, more than offsetting the increase in enrollment in all other private schools.[59]

The dramatic decline in Catholic commitment to parochial schooling, surely one of the most significant educational developments of the postwar era, was in part a response to the growing atmosphere of tolerance in public schools. The very developments that alienated many Protestants made the public school a far more attractive place to Catholics. The elimination of prayer and Bible-reading, the weakening of Protestant influence, and the growing acceptance of diversity made it possible for Catholic parents to send children to public schools without fearing either discrimination or the imposition of Protestant religious doctrines. The willingness of many large city school systems to provide released time for religious instruction in churches, a practice that became more common in the middle decades of the twentieth century, cinched the decision for a growing number of Catholic families.[60] Although the increasing moral laxity of the public schools was a persistent worry to Catholics, it was more than offset by a sense that public education no longer held a direct threat to the faith or dignity of their young.

As public schools became less hostile places for Catholic students, a number of demographic, social, and religious changes within American

Catholicism weakened support for parochial education. In part, parochial schools were the victims of Catholic success in American society. As children and grandchildren of immigrants found a place for themselves in the mainstream of American life, they felt less beleaguered and less in need of parochial education to protect their traditions in a hostile world. Similarly, Catholics who worked their way into the middle classes were more willing to abandon the parochial school. Often their upwardly mobile paths took them to the suburbs, where they were sometimes too spread out to sustain parochial schools. As substantial numbers of Catholics were able to escape their ethnic and working-class neighborhoods, they left behind struggling urban churches increasingly unable to bear the financial burdens of supporting parochial education for the desperately poor people who now occupied America's largest cities.[61]

Accompanying the social success of Catholics was a growing cultural and religious restiveness. Many Catholics shared in the general impatience with personal restraints in the postwar era, and they were increasingly willing to criticize the church's position on such issues as papal infallibility and artificial birth control. Especially after the Second Vatican Council, Catholics were less likely to attend church, less likely to abide by the church's sexual ethic, and less likely to accept key church doctrines. Although Catholics continued to hold parochial schools in high regard, they felt increasingly free to send their children to public school, leaving the task of religious education to special weekend and after-hours programs.

As the size and significance of the Catholic system declined, the character of the education it offered also changed. The most important development was the decline of traditional Catholic teaching orders and the increasing tendency of parochial schools to hire lay teachers. In the 1940s, fewer than 10 percent of the teachers were lay people; yet by 1965, the figure was 27 percent and by 1990 an astonishing 85 percent of teachers in Catholic schools were lay people.[62] The effect was to increase the cost of the schools (hastening the decline of the system) and to make it more difficult for them to offer sophisticated and informed instruction in religious doctrine.

The forces that led to a declining population of priests and nuns available to the parochial schools also contributed to a changing tone in the Catholic classroom. Scholars who have observed Catholic schools in the postwar era have noticed a less insistent approach to religious and moral education and a relaxation in the rules of student conduct. Yet Catholic educators have shown little interest in modern innovations in moral education. Catholics were among the first and most bitter critics of values clarification, and although Kohlberg has received a more tolerant reception, his ideas have also had relatively little effect on Catholic schools. For the most part, Catholic schools have continued to carry on an older tradition, integrating the religious with the moral and emphasizing the importance of transcendent and universal truths. Thus, despite its declining position in American education, the Catholic parochial system has continued to provide an important alternative tradition in moral education—a tradition that has in the past quarter of a century inspired imitation by groups that were once its bitterest critics.

Patterns of Change in Higher Education

By 1945 the decline of moral education was a well-established trend in colleges and universities. In the two decades that followed, the decline continued, slowly at first, then dramatically. The long-term trend was a product of a variety of forces, including the explosion of knowledge, the splintering of the curriculum, the creation of professional studies, the growing emphasis on research, and the influence of positivism. Nothing in the immediate postwar era worked to alter the impact of these forces and, in most respects, events of the 1940s and 1950s only accelerated the earlier trend. The growing prestige of science and technology, the military and economic competition with the Soviet Union, and the increasing demand for professional training all served to deepen commitments to research and specialization and, in the minds of many, to confirm the wisdom of positivism.

The reticence to provide moral education or even to engage in the serious discussion of values grew throughout the 1940s and 1950s on college and university campuses. As the prestige of scientific knowledge continued to rise, talk of morality seemed increasingly soft and sentimental. Social scientists found in the prosperity of the postwar years an affirmation of their positivism and talked hopefully about an end to ideology and the dawn of a world uncluttered by doctrine and moral dispute. The culture of the campus, like the culture of the wider society, still recognized the difference between heroic and contemptible behavior, but it forbade public discussion of the values that underlay such judgments and treated morality instead as a purely personal and private matter.[63]

The increasing absence of moral discourse on the college campus contributed to the growth of both skepticism and relativism among students. As Derek Bok, the former president of Harvard University, has pointed out, college life in these years did much to shatter the dogmas that students brought to campus but did little to help them reconstruct a more mature set of beliefs. "In a world in which so many norms were being challenged and student bodies were growing ever more diverse," wrote Bok, "educators found it hard to help inquiring undergraduates to replace their discarded dogmas with a new set of moral values. Instead, professors concentrated more and more on conveying knowledge and imparting skills, leaving students free to fashion their own beliefs and commitments amid the multiple distractions of campus life."[64] Lacking forums in which to test their values, students failed to acquire the capacity to judge ethical systems and developed instead a growing sense of moral relativism.

In the face of these developments, embattled defenders of moral education continued earlier efforts to stem the tide. For the most part they proceeded along lines that had been charted in the first four decades of the century. Progressives still argued for ethics courses that addressed normative questions and worked hard to promote the spread of special offerings to professional schools that had not responded to earlier urgings. In the 1950s their efforts received unexpected support from a growing interest in existentialism and religion. The work of such theorists as Jean-Paul Sartre, Martin Heidegger, Paul Tillich, Karl Barth, Martin Buber, and Richard and Reinhold Niebuhr gave a new impetus to the discussion of normative questions, and the dramatic growth of religion departments provided an array of scholars who, in this era at least, were eager to engage in discourse on the ethical issues of the day.

Champions of general education were also active in the 1940s and 1950s, continuing their efforts to use the humanities as a way to restore moral and civic education to the college and university. The starting point for their postwar activities was the report of a Harvard committee appointed by President James Conant to reexamine the role of general education in the undergraduate curriculum. The report, entitled *General Education in a Free Society*, was published in 1945.[65] Reflecting sentiments that would later appear in *Moral and Spiritual Values in the Public Schools*, the Harvard committee argued for a core of courses that would preserve basic American and Western values at a time when free, democratic societies were threatened by the specter of totalitarianism. Basically a moderate document, the report did not engage the fundamental issues raised by positivism or challenge the standing of scientific inquiry; instead it simply tried to preserve a balance in the curriculum and ensure that students would acquire the values considered essential to the survival of free society.

Despite their valiant efforts, defenders of moral education in colleges and universities remained on the defensive throughout the 1940s and 1950s. By the late 1960s they were in full-scale retreat. Not only had philosophical analysts finally captured the study of ethics, but as Douglas Sloan has pointed out, the undergraduate course had become "more isolated than ever within the college curriculum," an attractive offering only to "philosophy majors and the stray student from other fields seeking to fulfill a humanities requirement."[66] General education fared little better. Although the Harvard report had encouraged some tightening of distribution requirements, few institutions made serious efforts to create a well-integrated core of courses to provide moral and civic education. By the 1960s even the distribution requirements were weakened as colleges and universities sought to respond to every need for specialized training and every call for social relevance.

Accentuating these trends in the 1960s were many of the same forces that had led public schools to abandon moral education. Relativism was even more pervasive in higher education than in secondary and elementary schools, and it thwarted efforts to define a body of essential values or create a core of required courses. Similarly, distrust of authority and suspicion of rational discourse were rampant on college campuses, making it difficult for institutions to offer the kind of moral instruction that either the progressives or the supporters of general education sought to provide.

The intellectual and curricular chaos of the 1960s and 1970s left many old champions of ethics and liberal studies in dismay. Yet just beneath the stormy surface of campus life in those tumultuous years, normative questions were beginning to receive more serious consideration than they had in more than a generation. The very events that brought disorder to the campus—the civil rights movement, the war in Vietnam, concerns about the environment—also gave birth to a new vigor in moral discourse. Subsequent concerns about the conduct of public officials and about the ethical dilemmas facing professionals, especially in medicine, reinforced the emerging interest in moral questions.

The revival of moral discourse owed something to the efforts of both students and faculty. Student radicals of the 1960s and early 1970s broke sharply with the positivist ethos of the 1950s and portrayed political issues in stark, moral terms. Their demand for relevance in academic offerings, while leading to a further fragmentation of the curriculum, also resulted in the creation of classes that dealt with the most pressing moral issues of the day. Professors, perhaps drawing inspiration from their students, also began to show a new boldness in speaking to moral questions in both their research and their teaching. This was especially the case in ethics, where such figures as John Rawls and Robert Nozick defied the canons of philosophical analysis and wrote powerful works on fundamental normative questions.[67]

Although the decline of student radicalism and political controversy in the late 1970s and 1980s lowered the volume of moral debate in colleges and universities, ethical issues continued to receive a significant hearing in these decades. The most popular forums were courses in professional ethics, which had undergone a dramatic revival, and special classes on particular issues, such as the justifications for war, gender equity, and cultural pluralism. Unlike the traditional undergraduate ethics course, these classes were more likely to deal with practical dilemmas than with ethical theories and to engage a significantly broader range of students.

The revival of ethics in institutions of higher learning received important theoretical support from the research on moral development in the 1960s and 1970s. Of particular significance was the work of William G. Perry, Jr., which argued that the ethical development of college students moved through stages or "positions" from an "absolutistic right-wrong outlook" through an acceptance of relativism and finally to the development of mature commitment.[68] The work of Lawrence Kohlberg, though different in detail and focus, reinforced the notion of developmental stages and offered a powerful justification for the new emphasis on the discussion of practical dilemmas. Although Kohlberg's own reform efforts were focused on secondary schools, his theories applied equally well to moral education in the college years and did much to supply a rationale for the renewed emphasis on ethics.

As the study of ethics flourished on college campuses, most defenders of moral education took heart. Others, however, were skeptical. They saw in the modern ethics movement a subtle defense of relativism and called for a return to liberal studies. "The existence of 20,000 practical ethics courses," declared one critic, "does not mean we in the university are serious about the moral education of our students. If we were really serious, we would see that our students *all* got a substantial grounding in the liberal arts and sciences."[69] Even many supporters of the ethics movement saw it as only a first step in restoring moral education to the college campus. Harvard president Derek Bok, for example, believed that the study of ethics had to be combined with other activities, including "discussing rules of conduct with students and administering them fairly, building strong programs of community service, demonstrating high ethical standards in dealing with moral issues facing the university, and, finally, being more alert to the countless signals that institutions send to students and trying to make these messages support rather than undermine basic norms."[70]

Whatever the limitations of the new ethics courses, their emergence has been the single most important result of the effort to restore moral education to higher learning in the past quarter century. Other approaches have as yet borne little fruit. Surprisingly, champions of virtue-centered moral education have done far more to reform elementary and secondary programs than to revive the humanities in colleges and universities. Although they have been effective critics of the ethics movement, defenders of the humanities have done little to define a program of their own or to offer a realistic hope for a revival of general education. Their calls for a return to the study of the humanities have been vague and have left unanswered the questions that plagued earlier supporters of liberal culture and general education. Similarly, those who have sought to create a campus ethos that would encourage moral development have made only marginal advances since the 1960s. Although higher education in the 1980s and 1990s has been arguably more open to moral discourse than it had been in the 1950s, specific programs to cultivate character or encourage civic concern have been scattered at best. Except in church-affiliated colleges or in institutions with long traditions of social activism, campus life has continued to have far more to do with recreation than with moral development or community service.

The Present Moment in Moral Education

The effort to revive moral education is an ongoing revolution, and its outcome is far from clear at this point. At the level of elementary and secondary education, however, two generalizations can be made. First, the lines dividing particular groups of moral educators have become less sharp in recent years as theorists have tried to devise practical programs for the schools. Second, support for some form of moral education seems stronger at the century's end than at any time since the 1950s.

As champions of moral education have tried to devise specific programs for the schools in the 1990s, they have tended to blur the sharp theoretical distinctions that promoted such lively debate in the 1970s and 1980s. Sometimes blurring has been the product of deliberate efforts to compromise. Thus, in the summer of 1992, a group of disparate leaders came together in a conference sponsored by philanthropist Michael Josephson and endorsed a program centered around "the six pillars of character": trustworthiness, respect, responsibility, justice, caring, and civic virtue.[1] More often, however, the lines between the various schools of thought have been breached by practical reformers eager to endorse whatever programs might work to promote moral education. One of the most tireless champions of moral education, Thomas Lickona, for example, has been remarkably eclectic, endorsing just community schools, caring classrooms, traditional instruction in specific virtues, and a variety of other schemes.[2] Even Nel Noddings, who has done most to outline a specific feminist position on moral education, has acknowledged an important role for traditional instruction in the virtues.[3]

The spirit of accommodation and cooperation, though widespread, is not universal. A few theorists who have worked out of a progressive framework remain deeply suspicious of traditional moral education. Educator David E. Purpel, for example, sees the emphasis on personal virtues as a neoconservative strategy to divert attention from the needs for social reform. "The thrust of this approach," he writes, "is to move the discussion away from the extremely controversial realm of ideological dispute toward the safer and presumably more consensual realm of desirable personal traits, to convert social and political issues into educational and pedagogical ones, and to focus on stability rather than transformation."[4] At the other end of the spectrum, some conservative Christians continue to fear any form of moral education that does not root values in specific religious doctrines.[5]

Despite these continuing tensions, reformers have succeeded in winning substantial public support for moral education in the public schools. A number of states have passed legislation requiring some form of character education. For example, Indiana has mandated instruction that emphasizes such virtues as honesty, respect for the property of others, and personal responsibility to family and community. Many individual school systems, too, have developed guidelines for moral education, and there is ample evidence that a large number of schools across the country have either adopted special moral education programs or have made efforts to integrate moral instruction into the curriculum. Yet there is no systematic study to indicate just how deeply moral education has penetrated the daily life of the classroom and no evidence to suggest whether it has made a difference in the behavior of the young.[6] What does seem clear is that educators are less nervous about moral education than they were in the 1960s and 1970s and that they are more willing to respond to public pressure for a greater emphasis on matters of personal character.

The growing role of moral education in public schools, along with evidence of better discipline and more academic rigor, have deprived private education of some of its momentum. Yet some groups continue to believe that private schools can succeed where public schools have failed in the shaping of character. Scholarly studies that have argued the superiority of private schools in building character, in increasing academic performance, and even in achieving racial integration have given private education a new stature and have led a small circle of intellectual and political leaders to search for ways to offer public support to parents who preferred to send children to private schools. Although such proposals offer a viable policy option, there seems little reason to believe at this point that Americans will abandon their ancient commitment to a nonsectarian public schooling and entrust the moral education of their young to a diverse group of private institutions.

The current direction of moral education in colleges and universities is more difficult to discern. One heartening sign of progress to some supporters of moral education has been the recent revival of courses in ethics. Yet despite their popularity in professional schools, ethics courses have not found an entirely secure place in the undergraduate curriculum. Philosophy departments, to be sure, have continued to offer courses in ethics, but many of the new, issue-oriented classes have been staffed by professors from other fields. While the involvement of diverse disciplines has done much to enliven the study of ethics, it has also made the courses unusually vulnerable to changes in fashion. Without clear departmental sponsorship, the courses have depended heavily on the willingness of members of the faculty to venture beyond the usual disciplinary boundaries and to teach material that may have little to do with their research, a risky business in an academic world that still encourages specialization and expertise. Although ethics teachers have received impressive support from private foundations, especially the Hastings Center (or the Institute for Society, Ethics, and the Life Sciences), they have yet to build the kind of national professional societies that have been so critical to the success of other academic fields. The precarious place of ethics courses in contemporary colleges and universities is only one of the uncertainties facing those who seek to restore moral education to higher learning. The experience of the past quarter-century has provided little insight into the viability of other approaches. The resurrection of general education remains one option, but supporters have yet to articulate a specific program or to provoke a serious examination of the idea. The reinvigoration of campus life offers another possibility. Residential life programs that emphasize moral development or service learning have been proposed by a number of college and university leaders, and the emergence of professionals in student personnel administration make such programs conceivable even in an age when members of the faculty have little time to cultivate the character of their students. Yet this approach would require a significant redistribution of resources and a drastic change in the texture of student extracurricular life.

On balance, those who favor moral education in schools have been heartened by recent developments. Yet few have declared victory. However impressive the progress since the mid-1960s, moral education has yet to regain the place it had in the schools before the Second World War. Despite recent accommodations, educators have failed to build a broad consensus around any particular approach to moral education, and many programs remain controversial. Teachers receive almost no training in moral education from the nation's education schools and often struggle to find appropriate materials to use in the classroom. More important, the nature of public commitment to moral education is uncertain. It is possible for astute observers to see recent developments either as a return to normality after the aberrations of the 1960s and 1970s or as a temporary and largely symbolic response to several decades of youthful misbehavior that will disappear when the emergency is over. Whether Americans will seize the moment to restore moral education to the agenda of the nation's schools or lose their enthusiasm for the idea once again is beyond our ability to know. But few can doubt that the decision will be a fateful one.

Notes

Chapter 1

1. For a good brief treatment of Native American education in this era, see Margaret Connell Szasz, *Indian Education in the American Colonies, 1607–1783* (Albuquerque: University of New Mexico Press, 1988).

2. *The Diary of Samuel Sewall, 1674–1729*, ed. M. Halsey Thomas (New York: Farrar, Strauss and Giroux, 1973), 1:384. See also Charles E. Hambrick-Stowe, *The Practice of Piety: Puritan Devotional Discipline in Seventeenth-Century New England* (Chapel Hill: University of North Carolina Press, 1982); John Demos, *A Little Commonwealth: Family Life in Plymouth Colony* (London: Oxford University Press, 1970); Edmund Morgan, *The Puritan Family: Religion and Domestic Relations in Seventeenth-Century New England*, rev. ed. (New York: Harper and Row, 1966).

3. *The Diary of Cotton Mather, 1681–1708*, ed. Worthington Chauncey Ford, in Massachusetts Historical Society Collections, ser. 7, vol. 7 (Boston: The Society, 1911), 534. Entry is for February 1706.

4. Benjamin Wadsworth, "A Sermon, Setting Forth the Nature of Early Piety" in *A Course of Sermons on Early Piety by the Eight Ministers Who Carry on the Thursday Lecture in Boston* (Boston: n.p., 1721), 8.

5. "The Shorter Catechism, Agreed upon by the Reverend Assembly of Divines at Westminster in England," in *The New England Primer* (Boston: Manning and Loring, 1883), 26.

6. Ibid., 31–32.

7. See Ruth H. Bloch, "American Feminine Ideals in Transition: The Rise of the Moral Mother, 1785–1815," *Feminist Studies* 4 (June 1978): 101–126.

8. See Laurel Thatcher Ulrich, *Good Wives: Image and Reality in the Lives of Women in Northern New England, 1650–1750* (New York: Alfred A. Knopf, 1982).

9. See Helena M. Wall, *Fierce Communion: Family and Community in Early America* (Cambridge: Harvard University Press, 1990).

10. Nathaniel B. Shurtleff, ed., *Records of the Governor and Company of Massachusetts Bay, 1628–1686* (Boston: W. White, 1853–1854) 2:607.

11. For an extended account of the educational functions of the family, school, church, and apprenticeship, see Lawrence A. Cremin, *American Education: The Colonial Experience, 1607–1783* (New York: Harper and Row, 1970).

12. See Norman Fiering, *Moral Philosophy at Seventeenth-Century Harvard: A Discipline in Transition* (Chapel Hill: University of North Carolina Press, 1981); Frederick Rudolph, *The American College and University: A History* (New York: Random House, 1962).

13. Philip Greven, *The Protestant Temperament: Patterns of Child-Rearing, Religious Experience and the Self in Early America* (New York: New American Library, 1977); Richard P. Gildrie, *The Profane, the Civil and the Godly: The Reformation of Manners in Orthodox New England, 1649–1749* (University Park: Pennsylvania State University Press, 1994); David D. Hall, *Worlds of Wonder, Days of Judgment: Popular Religious Belief in Early New England* (Cambridge: Harvard University Press, 1989).

14. William W. Hening, ed., *The Statutes at Large: Being a Collection of all the Laws of Virginia from the First Session of the Legislature in the Year 1619* (Richmond: Samuel Pleasants Jr., 1809–1823), 1:157.

15. See Suzanne Lebsock, *"A Share of Honour": Virginia Women 1600–1945* (Richmond: Virginia Women's Cultural History Project, 1984); Kathleen M. Brown, *Good Wives, Nasty Wenches, and Anxious Patriarchs: Gender, Race, and Power in Colonial Virginia* (Chapel Hill: University of North Carolina Press, 1996); Darrett B. Rutman and Anita H. Rutman, *A Place in Time: Middlesex County, Virginia, 1650–1750* (New York: W. W. Norton, 1984).

16. See James Horn, *Adapting to a New World: English Society in the Seventeenth-Century Chesapeake* (Chapel Hill: University of North Carolina Press, 1994); Lois Green Carr, Russell R. Menard, and Lorena S. Walsh, *Robert Cole's World: Agriculture and Society in Early Maryland* (Chapel Hill: University of North Carolina Press, 1991).

17. See J. William Frost, *The Quaker Family in Colonial America: A Portrait of the Society of Friends* (New York: St. Martin's Press, 1973); Barry Levy, *Quakers and the American Family: British Settlement in the Delaware Valley* (New York: Oxford University Press, 1988).

18. See Michael Zuckerman, *Peaceable Kingdoms: New England Towns in the Eighteenth Century* (New York: Alfred A. Knopf, 1970).

19. See Karen Calvert, *Children in the House: The Material Culture of Early Childhood, 1600–1900* (Boston: Northeastern University Press, 1992); Jacqueline S. Reinier, *From Virtue to Character: American Childhood, 1775–1850* (New York: Twayne Publishers, 1996); Jay Fliegelman, *Prodigals and Pilgrims: The American Revolution against Patriarchal Authority, 1750–1800* (Cambridge: Cambridge University Press, 1982); Mary Beth Norton, *Founding Mothers and Fathers: Gendered Power and the Forming of American Society* (New York: Alfred A. Knopf, 1996); Patricia U. Bonomi, *Under the Cope of Heaven: Religion, Society and Politics in Colonial America* (New York: Oxford University Press, 1986).

20. See Greven, *Protestant Temperament*, chap. 6; Daniel Blake Smith, *Inside the Great House: Planter Family Life in Eighteenth-Century Chesapeake Society* (Ithaca, N.Y.: Cornell University Press, 1980).

21. See Bloch, "American Feminine Ideals."

22. Smith, *Inside the Great House*, p. 67.

23. For a fuller treatment, see B. Edward McClellan, "Public Education and Social Harmony: The Roots of an American Dream," *Educational Theory* 35 (Winter 1985): 33–42.

Chapter 2

1. Robert H. Wiebe, *The Opening of American Society: From the Adoption of the Constitution to the Eve of Disunion* (New York: Alfred A. Knopf, 1984).

2. For an excellent account of the interplay of freedom and restraint in political and educational thought, see Rush Welter, *Popular Education and Democratic Thought in America* (New York: Columbia University Press, 1962), pt. 2.

3. Richard J. Morris, "Urban Population Migration to Revolutionary America: The Case of Salem, Massachusetts, 1759–1799," *Journal of Urban History* 9 (November 1982): 3–30.

4. For an account of the decline of the family economy, see Mary P. Ryan, *Cradle of the Middle Class: The Family in Oneida County, New York, 1790–1865* (Cambridge: Cambridge University Press, 1981). See also John Mack Faragher, *Sugar Creek: Life on the Illinois Prairie* (New Haven: Yale University Press, 1986); Christopher Clark, *The Roots of Rural Capitalism, Western Massachusetts, 1780–1860* (Ithaca, N.Y.: Cornell University Press, 1990).

5. Horace Mann, untitled editorial, *The Common School Journal* 1 (November 1838): 14.

6. T. J. Biggs, "Lecture on Domestic Education," in *Transactions of the Fifth Annual Meeting of the Western Literary Institute and College of Professional Teachers, 1835* (Cincinnati: The Executive Committee, 1836), 52.

7. Emerson E. White, "Moral Training in the Public School," in *The Journal of Proceedings and Addresses of the National Education Association, 1886* (New York: NEA, 1887), 131.

8. Samuel G. Goodrich, *Fireside Education* (New York: F.J. Huntington, 1838), 72.

9. Daniel Drake, "Discourse on the Philosophy of Family, School and College Discipline," *Western Literary Institute Transactions, 1834*, 47.

10. Goodrich, 169–170.

11. See, for example, the advice offered by Lydia H. Sigourney, *Letters to Mothers* (Hartford, Conn.: Hudson and Skinner, 1838).

12. T. H. Gallaudet, *Child's Book of the Soul*, pts. 1 and 2 (Hartford: Cooke and Co., 1831); Lydia Sigourney, *The Boy's Book, Consisting of Original Articles in Prose and Poetry* (New York: Turner, Hughes, and Hayden, 1846).

13. For good general accounts of domestic education, see Anne L. Kuhn, *The Mother's Role in Childhood Education: New England Concepts, 1830–1860* (New Haven: Yale University Press, 1947); Jacqueline S. Reinier, *From Virtue to Character: American Childhood, 1775–1850* (New York: Twayne Publishers, 1996) and Bernard Wishy, *The Child and the Republic: The Dawn of Modern American Child Nurture* (Philadelphia: University of Pennsylvania Press, 1968), especially pt. 2.

14. See Anne M. Boylan, *Sunday School: The Formation of an American Institution, 1790–1880* (New Haven: Yale University Press, 1988). For a more extended treatment of the Sunday school, see chapter 3.

15. The growth of schooling is documented best in Carl F. Kaestle and Maris A. Vinovskis, *Education and Social Change in Nineteenth-Century Massachusetts* (Cambridge: Cambridge University Press, 1980).

16. For a full discussion, see Carl F. Kaestle, *Pillars of the Republic: Common Schools and American Society, 1780–1860* (New York: Hill and Wang, 1983).

17. George B. Emerson, "On the Education of Females," in *The Introductory Discourse and the Lectures Delivered Before the American Institute of Instruction, 1831* (Boston: Hilliard, Gray, Little, and Wilkins, 1832), 28.

18. Polly Welts Kaufman, *Women Teachers on the Frontier* (New Haven: Yale University Press, 1984), xviii.

19. Eli Tappan, "Examination of Teachers," *NEA Proceedings, 1883,* 7–8.

20. J. Orville Taylor, *The District School; Or National Education,* 3rd ed. (Philadelphia: Carey, Lea, and Blanchard, 1835), 114.

21. J. W. Stearns, "The Public Schools and Morality," *NEA Proceedings, 1885,* 89.

22. Ruth M. Elson, *Guardians of Tradition: American Schoolbooks of the Nineteenth Century* (Lincoln: University of Nebraska Press, 1964), 338.

23. William Holmes McGuffey, *McGuffey's Third Eclectic Reader,* 3rd rev. ed. (New York: American Book Co., 1896), 104–107.

24. David Riesman, et al., *The Lonely Crowd* (New Haven: Yale University Press, 1950).

25. Mann, untitled editorial, 49.

26. B. P. Aydelott, "Thoughts on American Education," *The Western Academician and Journal of Education and Science* 1 (July 1837): 257.

27. Kaestle, *Pillars of the Republic,* 106–107.

28. See William J. Reese, *The Origins of the American High School* (New Haven: Yale University Press, 1995).

29. See Frederick Rudolph, *The American College and University: A History* (New York: Vintage, 1962), especially chaps. 3–4.

30. For an excellent treatment of moral philosophy between the Revolution and the Civil War, see Wilson Smith, *Professors and Public Ethics: Studies of Northern Moral Philosophers Before the Civil War* (Ithaca, N.Y.: Cornell University Press, 1956).

31. For an account of student response to the new piety in higher education, see Rudolph, *The American College and University,* chaps. 4, 9.

Chapter 3

1. Horace Mann, comments in *Common School Journal* 3, no. 1, quoted by [Mary Mann], *The Life of Horace Mann,* 2nd ed. (Boston: Lee and Shepard, 1865), 142.

2. For an excellent account of the rise of nonsectarianism and many other matters discussed in this chapter, see Lloyd P. Jorgenson, *The State and the Non-*

Public School, 1825–1925 (Columbia: University of Missouri Press, 1987). See also the comprehensive study by Warren A. Nord, *Religion and American Education: Rethinking a National Dilemma* (Chapel Hill: University of North Carolina Press, 1995).

3. Heman Humphrey, "The Bible in Common Schools," *The Lectures Delivered Before the American Institute of Instruction, 1843* (Boston: William D. Ticknor, 1844): 10.

4. Harry S. McKeen, "The Ends of School Discipline," *Lectures of American Institute of Instruction, 1835*, p. 150.

5. Humphrey, "The Bible in Common Schools," 24.

6. See Anne M. Boylan, *Sunday School: The Formation of an American Institution, 1790–1880* (New Haven: Yale University Press, 1988).

7. Calvin E. Stowe, "Education of Immigrants," *Transactions of the Fifth Annual Meeting of the Western Literary Institute and College of Professional Teachers, 1835* (Cincinnati: The Institute, 1836), 66.

8. Horace Mann, *Twelfth Annual Report of the Board of Education together with the Twelfth Annual Report of the Secretary of the Board, 1848* (Boston: State Printer, 1849), 135; Horace Bushnell, *Common Schools: A Discourse on the Modifications Demanded by the Roman Catholics, Delivered in the North Church, Hartford, March 25, 1853*, reprinted in *American Writings on Popular Education*, ed. Rush Welter (Indianapolis: Bobbs-Merrill, 1971), 191; *Twelfth Annual Report on the Condition of the Common Schools to the City Council of Cincinnati, 1841* (Cincinnati: Daily Republic Office, 1841), 14–15.

9. F. Michael Perko, introduction to *Enlightening the Next Generation: Catholic and Their Schools, 1830–1890* (New York: Garland Publishing, 1988).

10. Jorgenson, *State and Non-Public School*, 74.

11. Ibid., 76–83.

12. "Acta et decreta concilii plenari Baltimorensis tertii," (Baltimore, 1886), reprinted in *Catholic Education in America: A Documentary History*, ed. Neil G. McCluskey (New York: Bureau of Publications, Teachers College, Columbia University, 1964), 94.

13. Bruce S. Cooper and Grace Dondero, "Survival, Change, and Demands on America's Private Schools: Trends and Policies," *Educational Foundations* 5 (Winter 1991): 57.

14. See Walter H. Beck, *Lutheran Elementary Schools in the United States: A History of the Developments of Parochial Schools and Synodical Educational Policies and Programs*, 2nd ed. (St. Louis: Concordia Publishing House, 1965).

15. Jon Diefenthaler, "Lutheran Schools in America," in *Religious Schooling in America*, ed. James C. Carper and Thomas C. Hunt (Birmingham, Ala.: Religious Education Press, 1984), 36, 41.

16. See James C. Carper, "The Christian Day School," in ibid., chap. 5; Susan D. Rose, *Keeping Them Out of the Hands of Satan: Evangelical Schooling in America* (New York: Routledge, 1988).

17. Paul A. Kienel, "The Forces Behind the Christian School Movement," *Christian School Comment* (1977): 1, quoted by Carper, "Christian Day School," 114.

18. Cooper and Dondero, "Survival, Change, and Demands," 63.

19. See Richard C. Hertz, *The Education of the Jewish Child: A Study of 200 Reform Jewish Religious Schools* (New York: Union of American Hebrew Congregations, 1953); Judah Pilch, ed., *A History of Jewish Education in America* (New York: American Association for Jewish Education, 1969).

20. Eduardo Rauch, "The Jewish Day School in America: A Critical History and Contemporary Dilemmas," in *Religious Schooling in America*, ed. Carper and Hunt, 142, 148.

21. *Pierce v Society of Sisters of Holy Name of Jesus and Mary* 268 U.S. 510 (1925). See David B. Tyack, "The Perils of Pluralism," *American Historical Review* 74 (October 1968): 74–98; Jorgenson, *State and Non-Public School*, chap. 10; Thomas C. Hunt and Norlene M. Kunkel, "Catholic Schools: The Nation's Largest Alternative School System," in *Religious Schooling in America*, ed. Carper and Hunt, 9.

22. Jorgenson, *State and Non-Public School*, 136–137.

Chapter 4

1. Thomas Bender, *Community and Social Change in America* (New Brunswick, N.J.: Rutgers University Press, 1978), 114. See also Robert H. Wiebe, *The Segmented Society: An Introduction to the Meaning of America* (New York: Oxford University Press, 1975).

2. Norfolk, Virginia, City School Board, Division of Research and Experimentation in Elementary Education, *Character Education in Norfolk Elementary Schools*, Bulletin No. 1 (Norfolk, Va.: City School Board, 1928), 17.

3. Oregon Office of the Superintendent of Public Instruction, *Character Education: A Manual for Oregon Teachers*, prepared by J. R. Jewell and R. C. Blackler (Salem, Ore.: State Printing Department, 1930), 12.

4. William J. Hutchins, *Children's Code of Morals for Elementary Schools* ([Washington: Character Education Institution, 1917]). This code was distributed as a four-page pamphlet, which may be found at the Library of Congress. It was widely reprinted, sometimes with minor modifications, in school board reports and educational journals. See, for example, Indiana Department of Public Instruction, *Bulletin No. 134: Character Education, Syllabus and Source Materials for Indiana Schools* (Indianapolis: Department of Public Instruction, 1942).

5. Birmingham Board of Education, *Something Better for Birmingham Children: The Story of Character Development in the Birmingham Public Schools* (Birmingham, Ala.: Board of Education, 1936); Boston Public Schools, *Character Education in Secondary Schools: Report of High School Head Masters' Association*, School Document No. 14, 1927 (Boston: Printing Department, 1928), esp. pp. 41, 104, 107.

6. Norfolk City School Board, *Character Education*, 104.

7. Educational News and Editorial Comment, *School Review* 47 (September 1939): 490.

8. Nebraska Department of Public Instruction, *A Course of Study in Character Education*, Supplementary Normal Training Bulletin, by F. M. Gregg (n.p.: Department of Public Instruction, [1927]), 129; Boston Public Schools *Annual Report of the*

Superintendent, School Document No. 10, 1926 (Boston: Printing Department, 1926), 13.

9. Nebraska Department of Public Instruction, *Course of Study in Character Education*, 132.

10. My understanding of the education of boys in this era is based heavily on the masterful unpublished paper "Boys Will Be Boys: Muscular Morality and the Curriculum of Adolescent Boyhood, 1900–1925," by David P. Setran of Indiana University.

11. Hugh Hartshorne and Mark A. May, *Studies in the Nature of Character*: Vol. 1, *Studies in Deceit*; Vol. 2, *Studies in Self-Control*; Vol. 3, *Studies in the Organization of Character* (New York: Macmillan, 1928–1930).

12. Charles B. Gilbert, "The Various Educational Demands upon the High School," *Educational Review* 23 (February 1902): 139.

13. Hugh Hartshorne, Character in Human Relations (New York: Charles Scribner's Sons, 1932), 208.

14. John Dewey, *Moral Principles in Education* (Boston: Houghton Mifflin Co., 1909), 58.

15. National Education Association, Department of Superintendence, *Tenth Yearbook: Character Education* (Washington, D.C.: Department of Superintendence, 1932), 11.

16. John Dewey, "Are the Schools Doing What People Want Them to Do?" *Educational Review* 21 (May 1901): 468–469; NEA, *Tenth Yearbook*, 37.

17. Ibid., 57.

18. National Education Association, *Report of the Committee on Character Education*, in U.S. Bureau of Education, Bulletin No. 7, 1926 (Washington: Government Printing Office, 1926), 1.

19. Dewey, *Moral Principles*, 43.

20. Hartshorne, *Character*, 21.

21. Hannah Arendt, "The Crisis in Education," in *Between Past and Future: Six Exercises in Political Thought* (New York: Viking Press, 1961), 181.

22. Michael Walzer, "The American School: Education for a Democratic Culture, I," *Dissent*, 6 (Spring 1959): 118.

23. Luke L. Mandeville, "The Catholic School and State Courses of Character Education," in *Character Education: A Symposium of Papers on Its Culture and Development*, ed. John M. Wolfe (New York: Benziger Brothers, 1930), 34.

24. For a masterful account of the changing place of moral education in colleges and universities around the turn of the century, see Julie A. Reuben, *The Making of the Modern University: Intellectual Transformation and the Marginalization of Morality* (Chicago: University of Chicago Press, 1996). See also George M. Marsden, *The Soul of the American University: From Protestant Establishment to Established Nonbelief* (New York: Oxford University Press, 1994).

25. James Branch Taylor, "College Education and Business," *Educational Review* 24 (March 1900): 248.

26. Reuben, *Making of a Modern University*.

27. For an excellent study of the developments in the teaching of ethics, see

Douglas Sloan, "The Teaching of Ethics in the American Undergraduate Curriculum, 1876–1976," in *The Teaching of Ethics in American Higher Education*, ed. Daniel Callahan and Sissela Bok (New York: Plenum Press, 1980), 1–57.

28. Bernard Rosen, "The Teaching of Undergraduate Ethics," in *The Teaching of Ethics*, ed. Callahan and Bok, 177.

29. See Lawrence R. Veysey, *The Emergence of the American University* (Chicago: Phoenix Books, 1965); Frederick Rudolph, *Curriculum: A History of the American Undergraduate Course of Study since 1636* (San Francisco: Jossey-Bass, 1978).

30. Sloan, "Teaching of Ethics," 42.

31. See Paula S. Fass, *The Damned and the Beautiful: American Youth in the 1920's* (Oxford: Oxford University Press, 1977); Helen Lefkowitz Horowitz, *Campus Life: Undergraduate Cultures from the End of the Eighteenth Century to the Present* (New York: Alfred A. Knopf, 1987); Christopher Jencks and David Riesman, *The Academic Revolution* (Garden City, N.Y.: Anchor Books, 1969); William C. Ringenberg, *The Christian College: A History of Protestant Higher Education in America* (Grand Rapids, Mich.: Christian University Press and William B. Eerdmans, 1984).

Chapter 5

1. Educational Policies Commission of the National Education Association and the American Association of School Administrators, *Moral and Spiritual Values in the Public Schools* (Washington: NEA, 1951), 17–20; 72–73.

2. Ibid., 52.

3. Henry Lester Smith, "A Program for Character Education," *Phi Delta Kappan* 31 (January 1950): 248–249. See also Henry Lester Smith, *Character Education: A Survey of Practice in the Public Schools of the United States* (Texarkana, Ark.-Tex.: Palmer Foundation, 1950).

4. Ernest M. Ligon, "Preparing Graduates of Church Related Colleges for Responsible Living with One's Fellow Man," *Christian Education* 30 (March 1947): 50; Ernest M. Ligon, *Dimensions of Character* (New York: Macmillan, 1956), ix.

5. For an excellent account of Ligon's involvement with Eli Lilly and the Lilly Endowment, see James H. Madison, *Eli Lilly: A Life, 1885–1977* (Indianapolis: Indiana Historical Society, 1989), 198–200.

6. For an early and particularly perceptive account of the declining moral authority of the public school, see Gerald Grant, "The Character of Education and the Education of Character," *Daedalus* 110 (Summer 1981): 135–149. See also Gerald Grant, *The World We Created at Hamilton High* (Cambridge: Harvard University Press, 1988); Theodore R. Sizer, *Horace's Compromise: The Dilemma of the American High School* (Boston: Houghton Mifflin, 1984); Arthur G. Powell, Eleanor Farrar, and David K. Cohen, *The Shopping Mall High School: Winners and Losers in the Educational Marketplace* (Boston: Houghton Mifflin Co., 1985).

7. Carl Bereiter, *Must We Educate?* (Englewood Cliffs, N.J.: Prentice-Hall, 1973), 36.

8. Robert Hampel, *The Last Little Citadel: American High Schools since 1940* (Boston: Houghton Mifflin, 1986), 94.

9. Raymond English, "The Revival of Moral Education," *American Education* 18 (January-February 1982): 4.

10. See Sizer, *Horace's Compromise*; Michael W. Sedlak et al., *Selling Students Short: Classroom Bargains and Academic Reform in the American High School* (New York: Teachers College Press, 1986).

11. See Grant, "The Character of Education."

12. Louis E. Raths, Merrill Harmin, and Sydney B. Simon, *Values and Teaching: Working with Values in the Classroom* (Columbus, Ohio: Charles E. Merrill, 1966); Howard Kirschenbaum, *Advanced Values Clarification* (La Jolla, Calif.: University Associates, 1977).

13. Raths, Harmin, and Simon, *Values and Teaching*, 5.

14. Ibid., 10.

15. Ibid., 7.

16. Ibid., 28–29.

17. Ibid., 53, 193.

18. Alan L. Lockwood, "A Critical View of Values Clarification," *Teachers College Record* 77 (September 1975): 40.

19. Kenneth A. Strike, "The Legal and Moral Responsibility of Teachers," in *The Moral Dimensions of Teaching*, ed. John I. Goodlad, Roger Soder, and Kenneth A. Sirotnik (San Francisco: Jossey-Bass, 1990), 211.

20. William Casement, "Moral Education: Form without Content?" *Educational Forum* 48 (Winter 1984): 181.

21. Andrew Oldenquist, "Moral Education without Moral Education," *Harvard Educational Review* 49 (May 1979): 242.

22. Lawrence Kohlberg, "The Quest for Justice in 200 Years of American History and in Contemporary American Education," *Contemporary Education* 48 (Fall 1976): 6.

23. Howard Muson, "Moral Thinking: Can It Be Taught?" *Psychology Today* 12 (February 1979): 51.

24. Lawrence Kohlberg, "Moral Education in the Schools: A Developmental View," *School Review* 74 (Spring 1966): 7.

25. Ibid., 9; Lawrence Kohlberg, "Moral Education for a Society in Moral Transition," *Educational Leadership* 33 (October 1975): 46–54.

26. Lawrence Kohlberg, "Moral Development and the New Social Studies," *Social Education* 37 (May 1973): 374–375.

27. Kohlberg, "Moral Education for a Society," 50.

28. Ibid.

29. Kevin Ryan, *Questions and Answers on Moral Education*, Fastback No. 53 (Bloomington, Ind.: Phi Delta Kappa Educational Foundation, 1981), 24. See also David C. McClelland, "What Behavioral Scientists Have Learned about How Children Learn Values," in *The Development of Social Maturity*, ed. David C. McClelland (New York: Irvington, 1982), 25–26; Howard Muson, "An Overview of Educational Efforts to Improve Character," in *Education for Values*, ed. David C. McClelland (New York: Irvington, 1982), 15; Strike, "Legal and Moral Responsibility," 213.

30. Lawrence Kohlberg, "Moral Education Reappraised," *The Humanist* 38 (November 1978): 14.

31. Ibid.

32. Oldenquist, "Moral Education," 243.

33. Carol Gilligan, *In a Different Voice: Psychological Theory and Women's Development* (Cambridge: Harvard University Press, 1982), 22; 69–70; 73; 101.

34. Ibid., 74. See also Carol Gilligan, Jamie Victoria Ward, and Jill McLean Taylor, eds., *Mapping the Moral Domain* (Cambridge: Harvard University Press, 1988).

35. Nel Noddings, *Caring: A Feminine Approach to Ethics and Moral Education* (Berkeley: University of California Press, 1984), 1.

36. Nel Noddings, "A Morally Defensible Mission for Schools in the 21st Century," *Phi Delta Kappan* 76 (January 1995): 367. See also Jane Roland Martin, *The Schoolhome: Rethinking Schools for Changing Families* (Cambridge: Harvard University Press, 1992).

37. Nel Noddings, "Teaching Themes of Care," *Phi Delta Kappan* 76 (May 1995): 675. See also Eric Schaps, Victor Rattistich, and Daniel Solomon, "School as a Caring Community: A Key to Character Education," in *The Construction of Children's Character*, Ninety-Sixth Yearbook of the National Society for the Study of Education, pt. 2, ed. Alex Molnar (Chicago: University of Chicago Press, 1997), 127–139.

38. Ray S. Erlandson Sr., "A Curriculum for Character Education," *Principal* 65 (January 1986): 32; Russell C. Hill, "Freedom's Code," *Character Education Journal* 2 (Spring-Summer 1973), n.p.

39. Erlandson, "A Curriculum," 32; Frank G. Goble and B. David Brooks, *The Case for Character Education* (Ottawa, Ill.: Green Hill, 1983), 99.

40. Erlandson, "A Curriculum," 32.

41. George C. S. Benson, "American Ethics and Independent Schools," *Independent School Bulletin* 33 (May 1974): 14.

42. Bill Honig, *Last Chance for Our Children: How You Can Help Save Our Schools* (Reading, Mass.: Addison-Wesley, 1985), 106.

43. Oldenquist, "Moral Education," 246.

44. Honig, *Last Chance*, 102.

45. William J. Bennett, "Moral Literacy and the Formation of Character," *NASSP Bulletin* 72 (December 1988): 31.

46. Ibid., 33.

47. William J. Bennett, ed., *The Book of Virtues: A Treasury of Great Moral Stories* (New York: Simon and Schuster, 1993). For another collection designed to promote moral behavior, see Colin Greer and Herbert Kohl, eds., *A Call to Character* (New York: Harper Collins, 1995).

48. Bennett, "Moral Literacy and the Formation of Character," 35.

49. Honig, *Last Chance*, 105.

50. Bruce S. Cooper and Grace Dondero, "Survival, Change, and Demands on America's Private Schools: Trends and Policies," *Educational Foundations* 5 (Winter 1991): 57.

51. See Pearl R. Kane, "Independent Schools in American Education," *Teacher*

College Record 92 (Spring 1991): 396–407; Arthur G. Powell, *Lessons from Privilege: The American Prep School Tradition* (Cambridge: Harvard University Press, 1996).

52. Susan D. Rose, *Keeping Them Out of the Hands of Satan: Evangelical Schooling in America* (New York: Routledge, 1988), 36.

53. Cooper and Dondero, "Survival, Change, and Demands," 63. See also James C. Carper, "The Christian Day School," in *Religious Schooling in America*, ed. James C. Carper and Thomas C. Hunt (Birmingham, Ala.: Religious Education Press, 1984); William J. Reese, "The Public Schools and the Great Gates of Hell," *Educational Theory* 32 (Winter 1982): 9–17.

54. Tim LaHaye, *The Battle for the Public Schools: Humanism's Threat to Our Children* (Old Tappan, N.J.: Fleming H. Revell, 1983), 240.

55. Paul A. Kienel, *The Christian School: Why It Is Right for Your Child* (Wheaton, Ill.: Victor Books, 1977), 71. Kienel is incorrect in identifying Dewey as the head of Teachers College. Dewey's primary appointment at Columbia was in the philosophy department.

56. See George Ballweg, "The Growth in the Number and Population of Christian Schools since 1966: A Profile of Parental Views Concerning Factors Which Led Them to Enroll Their Children in a Christian School" (Ph.D. diss., Boston University, 1980); Rose, *Keeping Them Out*, 33.

57. Kienel, *The Christian School*, 15.

58. For a description of two Christian schools with decidedly different climates, see Rose, *Keeping Them Out*.

59. Cooper and Dondero, "Survival, Change, and Demands," 57.

60. Although the Supreme Court ruled in *McCollum v Board of Education* (1948) that it was unconstitutional to provide released time for religious activities inside public schools, the decision did not prevent schools from releasing students for instruction off the school grounds.

61. See Glen Gabert, *In Hoc Signo? A Brief History of Catholic Parochial Education in America* (Port Washington, N.Y.: Kennikat Press, 1973); Harold A. Buetow, *Of Singular Benefit: The Story of U.S. Catholic Education* (New York: Macmillan, 1970); Thomas C. Hunt and Norlene M. Kunkel, "Catholic Schools: The Nation's Largest Alternative School System," in *Religious Schooling in America*, ed. Carper and Hunt, 1–34; Andrew M. Greeley, William C. McGready, and Kathleen McCourt, *Catholic Schools in a Declining Church* (Kansas City: Sheed and Ward, 1976). I am grateful to Patricia A. Bauch of the University of Alabama for sharing an unpublished paper on Catholic education.

62. Statistics provided by Patricia A. Bauch; see also Michael J. Guerra, *Lighting New Fires: Catholic Schooling in America 25 Years after Vatican II* (Washington, D.C.: National Catholic Education Association, 1991), 6.

63. For a particularly astute comment on the privatization of values in American culture, see Michael Walzer, "Teaching Morality," *New Republic* 178 (June 10, 1978): 12–14.

64. Derek Bok, *Universities and the Future of America* (Durham, N.C.: Duke University Press, 1990), 70.

65. *General Education in a Free Society: Report of the Harvard Committee* (Cambridge: Harvard University Press, 1945).

66. Douglas Sloan, "The Teaching of Ethics in the American Undergraduate Curriculum, 1876–1976," in *The Teaching of Ethics*, ed. Daniel Callahan and Sissela Bok, 40.

67. John Rawls, *A Theory of Justice* (Cambridge: Harvard University Press, 1971); Robert Nozick, *Anarchy, State, and Utopia* (New York: Basic Books, 1974).

68. William G. Perry Jr., *Forms of Intellectual and Ethical Development in the College Years* (New York: Holt, Rinehart, and Winston, 1968), chap. 5.

69. Robert K. Fullinwider, *Teaching Ethics in the University* (Bloomington, Ind.: The Poynter Center, 1991), 6.

70. Bok, *Universities*, 97.

Epilogue

1. William Barnhill, "Speak up for 'Character.'" *AARP Bulletin* 37 (February 1995): 19.

2. Thomas Lickona, "Educating for Character: A Comprehensive Approach," in *The Construction of Children's Character*, Ninety-Sixth Yearbook of the National Society for the Study of Education, pt. 2, ed. Alex Molnar (Chicago: University of Chicago Press, 1997), 45–62. See also Howard Kirschenbaum, "A Comprehensive Model for Values Education and Moral Education," *Phi Delta Kappan* 73 (June 1992): 771–776; William Damon, *The Moral Child: Nurturing Children's Natural Moral Growth* (New York: Free Press, 1988); Thomas Lickona, *Educating for Character: How Our Schools Can Teach Respect and Responsibility* (New York: Bantam Books, 1991).

3. Nel Noddings, "Character Education and Community," in *Construction of Children's Character*, 10.

4. David Purpel, "The Politics of Character Education," in *Construction of Children's Character*, 140. See also Alan L. Lockwood, "Character Education: The Ten Percent Solution," *Social Education* 55 (April-May 1991): 246–248.

5. Barbara B. Gaddy, T. William Hall, and Robert J. Marzano, *School Wars: Resolving Our Conflicts over Religion and Values* (San Francisco: Jossey-Bass, 1996).

6. See James S. Leming, "Research and Practice in Character Education: A Historical Perspective," in *Construction of Children's Character*, 31–44.

Suggested Reading

Bennett, William J. "Moral Literacy and the Formation of Character." *NASSP Bulletin* 72 (December 1988): 29–34.

Bennett, William J., and Edwin J. Delattre. "Moral Education in the Schools." *Public Interest* 50 (Winter 1978): 82–92.

Bloch, Ruth H., "American Feminine Ideals in Transition, 1785–1815." *Feminist Studies* 4 (June 1978): 101–126.

Bok, Derek. *Universities and the Future of America.* Durham, N.C.: Duke University Press, 1990.

Boylan, Anne M. *Sunday School: The Formation of an American Institution, 1790–1880.* New Haven: Yale University Press, 1988.

Buetow, Harold A. *Of Singular Benefit: The Story of U.S. Catholic Education.* New York: Macmillan, 1970.

Calvert, Karen. *Children in the House: The Material Culture of Early Childhood, 1600–1900.* Boston: Northeastern University Press, 1992.

Carper, James C., and Thomas C. Hunt, eds. *Religious Schooling in America.* Birmingham, Ala.: Religious Education Press, 1984.

Casement, William. "Moral Education: Form without Content?" *Educational Forum* 48 (Winter 1984): 177–189.

Coles, Robert. *The Moral Life of Children.* Boston: Houghton Mifflin, 1986.

Cooper, Bruce S., and Grace Dondero, "Survival, Change, and Demands on America's Private Schools: Trends and Policies." *Educational Foundations* 5 (Winter 1991): 51–74.

Cremin, Lawrence A. *American Education: The Colonial Experience, 1607–1783.* New York: Harper and Row, 1970.

Damon, William. *The Moral Child: Nurturing Children's Natural Moral Growth.* New York: Free Press, 1988.

Demos, John. *A Little Commonwealth: Family Life in Plymouth Colony.* Chapel Hill: University of North Carolina Press, 1970.

Elson, Ruth M. *Guardians of Tradition: American Schoolbooks of the Nineteenth Century.* Lincoln: University of Nebraska Press, 1964.

Frost, J. William. *The Quaker Family in Colonial America: A Portrait of the Society of Friends.* New York: St. Martin's Press, 1973.

Gabert, Glen. *In Hoc Signo? A Brief History of Catholic Parochial Education in America.* Port Washington, N.Y.: Kennikat Press, 1973.

Gaddy, Barbara B., T. William Hall, and Robert J. Marzano, *School Wars: Resolving Our Conflicts over Religion and Values*. San Francisco: Jossey-Bass, 1996.

Gilligan, Carol. *In a Different Voice: Psychological Theory and Women's Development*. Cambridge: Harvard University Press, 1982.

Grant, Gerald. "The Character of Education and the Education of Character." *Daedalus* 110 (Summer 1981): 135–149.

Greven, Philip. *The Protestant Temperament: Patterns of Child-Rearing, Religious Experience and the Self in Early America*. New York: New American Library, 1977.

Guerra, Michael J. *Lighting New Fires: Catholic Schooling in America 25 Years after Vatican II*. Washington, D.C.: National Catholic Education Association, 1991.

Jorgenson, Lloyd P. *The State and the Non-Public School, 1825–1925*. Columbia: University of Missouri Press, 1987.

Kane, Pearl R. "Independent Schools in American Education." *Teachers College Record* 92 (Spring 1991): 396–407.

Kilpatrick, William. *Why Johnny Can't Tell Right from Wrong*. New York: Simon and Schuster, 1992.

Kohlberg, Lawrence. "Moral Education in the Schools: A Developmental View." *School Review* 74 (Spring 1966): 1–30.

———. "Moral Education Reappraised." *The Humanist* 38 (November 1978): 13–15.

———. "Moral Education for a Society in Moral Transition." *Educational Leadership* 33 (October 1975): 46–54.

———. "The Quest for Justice in 200 Years of American History and in Contemporary American Education." *Contemporary Education* 48 (Fall, 1976): 5–16.

Kuhn, Anne L. *The Mother's Role in Childhood Education: New England Concepts, 1830–1860*. New Haven: Yale University Press, 1947.

LaHaye, Tim. *The Battle for the Public Schools: Humanism's Threat to Our Children*. Old Tappan, N.J.: Fleming H. Revell, 1983.

Marsden, George M. *The Soul of the University: From Protestant Establishment to Established Nonbelief*. New York: Oxford University Press, 1994.

Molnar, Alex, ed. *The Construction of Children's Character*. Ninety-Sixth Yearbook of the National Society for the Study of Education, pt. 2. Chicago: University of Chicago Press, 1997.

Morgan, Edmund. *The Puritan Family: Religion and Domestic Relations in Seventeenth-Century New England*. Rev. ed. New York: Harper and Row, 1966.

Noddings, Nel. *Caring: A Feminine Approach to Ethics and Moral Education*. Berkeley: University of California Press, 1984.

Nord, Warren A. *Religion & American Education: Rethinking a National Dilemma*. Chapel Hill: University of North Carolina Press, 1995.

Oldenquist, Andrew. "Moral Education without Moral Education." *Harvard Educational Review* 49 (May 1979): 240–247.

Perko, F. Michael. *Enlightening the Next Generation: Catholics and Their Schools, 1830–1890.* New York: Garland Publishing, 1988.

Perry, William G. Jr. *Forms of Intellectual and Ethical Development in the College Years.* New York: Holt, Rinehart, and Winston, 1968.

Raths, Louis E., Merrill Harmin, and Sydney B. Simon, *Values and Teaching: Working with Values in the Classroom.* Columbus, Ohio: Charles E. Merrill, 1966.

Reinier, Jacqueline S. *From Virtue to Character: American Childhood, 1775–1850.* New York: Twayne Publishers, 1996.

Reuben, Julie A. *The Making of the Modern University: Intellectual Transformation and the Marginalization of Morality.* Chicago: University of Chicago Press, 1996.

Ringenberg, William G. *The Christian College: A History of Protestant Higher Education in America.* Grand Rapids, Mich.: Christian University Press and William B. Eerdmans, 1984.

Rose, Susan D. *Keeping Them Out of the Hands of Satan: Evangelical Schooling in America.* New York: Routledge, 1988.

Sloan, Douglas. "The Teaching Ethics in the American Undergraduate Curriculum, 1876–1976." In *The Teaching of Ethics in American Higher Education,* ed. Daniel Callahan and Sissela Bok. New York: Plenum Press, 1980, 1–57.

Smith, Daniel Blake. *Inside the Great House: Planter Family Life in Eighteenth-Century Chesapeake Society.* Ithaca, N.Y.: Cornell University Press, 1980.

Smith, Wilson. *Professor and Public Ethics: Studies of Northern Moral Philosophers Before the Civil War.* Ithaca, N.Y.: Cornell University Press, 1956.

Veysey, Lawrence R. *The Emergence of the American University.* Chicago: Phoenix Books, 1965.

Wishy, Bernard. *The Child and the Republic: The Dawn of Modern American Child Nurture.* Philadelphia: University of Pennsylvania Press, 1968.

Index

About the Author

B. EDWARD MCCLELLAN is Professor of Education and American Studies and acting chair of the Department of Educational Leadership and Policy Studies at Indiana University. He has served as associate editor and acting editor of the *Journal of American History* and editor of the *History of Education Quarterly.*